"The Art of Telephone Selling" ISBN 0 9519019 0 7 (out of pri
©Brenda Spiller first printed 1995 by

Charles Books Co.
Canada House
272 Field End Road
Eastcote
Ruislip HA4 9NA

Tel: 020 8582 0367
Fax: 020 8866 3725
Email: info@charlesbooksco.co.uk

"Perfecting The Art Of Telesales *Spiced With The Magic Of Neuro-Linguistic Programming*" ISBN 0 9519019 5 8 (revised and enlarged edition) © Brenda Spiller 2003

Edited by Jennifer Thomas, USA.

Second reprint, January 2006

British Library Cataloguing in Publication Data

A catalogue record for this book is available from the British Library.

Visit the Charles Books Website at: www.charlesbooksco.co.uk

Foreword

What terrifies many, many professionals? The idea of picking up the phone to sell to people they do not know. "What will I say? How do I begin the conversation? No one buys over the phone anyway. Either no one is ever in the office or you can't get through all the roadblocks to the decision-maker. I hate telemarketers and I certainly don't want to be like them!"

These are some of the thoughts stopping skilled people from earning a decent living in their chosen profession. "Sales reluctance" as it is often called, may soon be listed as a new mental illness. People cope with sales reluctance in different ways. Some align themselves with someone else they hope will do the selling for them. Some do nothing. Some burst into a spasm of phoning people to no avail and then give up. Some repeat their mantra over and over; "The universe will provide " waiting for a miracle. Rarely have any of these strategies created or sustained a business for long.

Brenda Spiller has been helping people increase their telesales since 1984. Before that Brenda made her living on the telephone and then running telesales operations. She has seen and dealt with every issue that faces people who work on the phone.

In this book she approaches telesales in a step-by-step manner, taking beginners or seasoned professionals through everything you need to know. Her suggestions for prospecting (the art of reaching the people who have a need and the resources to purchase what you are selling) are excellent. There are many helpful tips, tactics and forms to organize your approach. She always has an answer to that nagging question: "But what would I say if the customer says/does…?" And she even has a technique to help adjust your emotional state to get in the right frame of mind for telesales.

Brenda has also integrated the models from Neuro-Linguistic Programming to dramatically improve how you communicate with your prospects and customers. She demonstrates building rapport and credibility, below conscious motivation strategies and specific language patterns for selling.

This book has something for everyone who earns his or her living through telesales.

Shelle Rose Charvet
Author of "Words That Change Minds: Mastering the Language of Influence"

How this guidebook is organized

Contents: **Pages**

PART FOUR
Telephone Selling

PART FIVE
Adding spice

Perfecting The Art Of Telesales Spiced With The Magic Of Neuro-Linguistic Programming

PART SIX
Focus on success

PART SEVEN
Forms and Book list

Self organization and monitoring records:

About the Author: Brenda Spiller

1972 was Brenda's first introduction to telephone selling. Working in the telephone sales section of a fastenings company, selling nuts, bolts and screws over the telephone. A riveting job – pardon the pun! However, it was the start of what has proved to be an interesting and exciting career.

This was followed by a couple of years in British Telecom. Then onto the UK's largest safety organisation where Brenda ran a Telephone Sales team of 28 persons. Her role and responsibilities included the planning and selling of courses, and training of the telesales force. Generating revenues in excess £1.3 million per year this organisation was training over 26,000 people per annum on both public and on-site safety courses worldwide.

In 1984 she set up a telemarketing, consultancy and training business - B's Management Services. After a period of almost meteoric growth, she split the company so that the on-site telemarketing would develop in its own right and this became B's Telemarketing Ltd. Brenda continued to work as an international business consultant and trainer, as well as remaining a major shareholder and chairman of the telemarketing business.

In 6 years the telemarketing organisation had grown from 2 to 35 telemarketers, it was attractive enough to be sold at a substantial profit to the largest US direct marketing company with interests in the UK. This placed Brenda in the enviable position of being able to follow her real passion and concentrate her energies on call-centre consultancy, customer service improvement, sales and communication skills training. She set up Shine Consultancy & Training Ltd.

Shine designs and conducts a wide variety of training programmes - all provided in-house to accommodate a company's real needs and to ensure they conform with organisational culture.

Brenda still facilitates programmes where inspiration and motivation, (i.e. more than behaviour training per se) is required to help people reach their goals and achieve peak performance in a demanding and competitive environment. She loves helping people grow and develop using her unique, very upbeat high-energy style of coaching, facilitating or training. She is a Certified Trainer of Neuro-Linguistic Programming and acts as mentor to people just starting out in business.

She knows that appropriate training is not always available to those choosing a career in telephone selling, or who are just getting started in a business of their own. Time and funds may not be available either to take courses to learn the art of Telephone Selling.

The **purpose of this guidebook,** and others that are available, is to:

-   Bring 'telephone selling' knowledge and techniques to you, so you can learn and develop your skills in a simple, practical and cost effective way.

-   Provide inspiration and motivation, to help you reach your telephone sales goals and achieve peak performance in a demanding and competitive world.

During her own years of development Brenda was given a 15-word sales course, which summarizes the art of salesmanship:

-   *Know your product*
-   *Believe in it*
-   *Call (visit) a lot of people*
-   *Ask all of them to buy*

If you want to play the numbers game, this is certainly one way to achieve success, and for some people, and with certain products, this may be a very easy and successful way of achieving quantity sales – it does not necessarily achieve quality.

Brenda knows that for most of us it is more complex than this, and the psychology and structure of the telephone sales process needs to be fully understood and put into effect and practised.

Because, if telephone selling were as easy as that 15-word course suggests, training and information would not be necessary, and everyone in sales would always be successful - and this is not so.

Brenda trusts that this guidebook will help you grow and develop your skills to ensure you achieve the success you desire and deserve.

"My guidebook is dedicated to you. I wish you continuing success and happiness in all that you do in life. You will discover that the universe is abundant – just believe".

Brenda Spiller

Brenda Spiller

Notes from the author

There are many books written on selling and marketing all of which have great value. I have read many, and they have, and still do, assist me in my personal development - no one ever stops learning!

However, when I was young and developing my skills I often really wanted books specific to my chosen profession - telephone selling, and preferably for that knowledge to come from someone who had actually followed this career. In my early days, this was a tall order. Today this is not the case; I am one of many who have chosen this career, however, I may be one of the few who has dedicated a lifetime's work training others to be successful at telephone selling.

Personality, as you know, has much to do with successful telephone selling; people buy from people they like. Integrity, honesty, sincerity and truth are also essential ingredients in this profession.

It is vital that you be happy pursuing a telephone selling profession. If you are the type of person who loses heart easily, then it may be better to choose a less demanding career.

Most people, including experienced sales people, intensely dislike telephone cold calling and prospecting because they fear failure. The degree to which you may appear to experience more rejection over the telephone than if you choose a career in field sales, occurs simply because it is possible to make more phone calls than it is field sales visits. Therefore, the proportion of calls vs. visits is much higher, and of course the prospects pay no mind as to how their rejection or rudeness over the phone can affect your emotional state - if you choose to let it!

The prospect is rejecting the call, not you. It is not personal.

- His intention - not to take your call right now.

- His behaviour – gruff or negative tone, sharp retort, inappropriate statement "I'm not interested" (when he hasn't heard anything other than your name and company name), and possibly slamming down the phone.

- He could have chosen a different and positive behaviour - diverted his call, not picked up the phone at all, answered it politely and listened, and then said he is "not interested" or asked you to call at another time. His intention would be the same, i.e. not to take your call right now, but his behaviour is very different.

Once you can learn to 'separate intention from behaviour' you will view these situations quite differently and handle them yourself more calmly. Please be assured I am not condoning his poor behaviour, I am just pointing out another way of looking at it.

If of course you were face to face with the prospect he would not behave in such a manner. So start to recognise 'people have behaviour that is not who they are'. He is a lovely prospect trying to get out from behind his poor behaviour.

However, you have chosen telephone selling so learn to 'be at cause'! (see p. 23.)

Fear of rejection is one of the biggest obstacles to success. Telephone selling puts your ego on the line and you become terrified of the word 'no!'. Nothing is ever as terrible as it seems. Your thoughts and beliefs are often unrealistic, and nothing that happens is terrible unless you allow your thoughts to convince you they are. And, who said things should, ought or must happen.

The reason why your thoughts and beliefs make you emotional is because they mismatch between what you **believe** should happen and what is happening!

The obvious way to avoid failure is never to try at all.

- Don't pick up the telephone
- Don't call prospects
- Don't make powerful presentations
- Don't close that business deal

The dedicated telesales person knows that rejection comes with the territory; there is nothing personal about it, and you cannot expect success every time.

There is no failure, there is only feedback, so pay attention to the feedback and use it to your advantage. Change what is not working. Keep what is.

What you need to understand is that there are other opportunities awaiting you, that you are continuously learning from the rejection, and that you never allow the setback to dim your enthusiasm. The more NOs the closer to YES you are getting.

You cannot win in any game without entering it.

When you care about what you are doing you will naturally be a little anxious and excited about the outcome. Anxiety is a fear of the future – so whatever is concerning you has not yet happened - it is all in your mind, so think differently and plan your future.   And, if you are the type of person who likes to worry, and still chooses to do so, then at least do it constructively, which means looking ahead at every step of the sale to see what may not go your way, and work out what you will do when it doesn't.

See all telesales calls, and in particular rejection, as a challenge, and an opportunity to improve your skill.

This guidebook does not have all the answers, but it has some along with tried and tested techniques. Not just tested by myself, but by all the people I have successfully trained over the last two decades.

Successful telephone sales people put their own flair into telephone selling. Therefore, just like them, you can add a variety of other ideas to these techniques. So find out what works for you, and use it. Remembering, however, that it is important to be courteous, sincere, confident, positive, cheerful, and focused – always stay focused.

Keep pace with changing attitudes towards telephone selling and you will make profitable sales.

Be ruthless in your assessment of yourself, pay attention to your telephone sales presentation, and continuously improve upon it. The only way to learn effective and profitable telephone selling is to practice, pay attention, keep what works, discard what doesn't; practise, pay attention, keep what works, discard what doesn't, and more practise. Make many quality calls and often. Decide that every day will be exciting and fun.

Thank you for investing in this guidebook. May it serve you well in your telephone selling endeavours.

Note: "he" has been used throughout as a substitute for "he/she" in the interests of maintaining the flow of the text and immediacy of the message.

Acknowledgements

It would be wonderful to weave you a tall tale of sitting up late at night, peering at my PC screen with writer's block and lack of inspiration. The reality is very different.

This guidebook is in part some of my lifetime's work, and in my lifetime many people have inspired me. All of them contributed to this guide in one way or another, so I would like universally to acknowledge and thank all sources from which this material originated, giving me the opportunity to share it with you.

This guidebook is the product of many minds; some of the people I have never met but reading their books and articles, or listening to them at courses and conferences provided me with some profound knowledge and insight. It is also the product of personal experience – the making of telephone sales calls to all those unsuspecting prospects and customers; and of course the minds of the people I have had the pleasure of training over the last 20+ years.

So, first, I must thank the dozens of prospects and customers that I have practised my calls on. And, second, the hundreds of course participants I had the pleasure of meeting through my loyal customers, who have invested in my telesales training programmes over the years.

The results of those years of training and the continuous feedback I received have created the words that appear on these pages.

For the production of the guidebook itself I must give my gratitude to my friend Jenny, in New York, who lent valuable assistance, and countless hours, in editing my drafts.

My friend Jacquie, who allowed me to 'model' her as the most excellent telesales person I know and to tap her subconscious to provide some valuable insight into telephone selling.

My friend Helen gave me my first opportunity to become a professional telesales person – I shall forever be indebted to her.

My daughter Karen, son-in-law Stewart and grandchildren Ruby and Lewis for their moral support.

Finally, all those who have given so much to the world through Neuro-Linguistic Programming (NLP):

Richard Bandler & John Grinder, the co-developers of NLP
Tad James
And many others, too numerous to mention.

Shelle Rose Charvet, who not only provided permission to use some of her valuable work, but also kindly lent her name in support of this book.

Thank you all.

Part one

Introduction
&
Definitions

"Perfecting The Art Of Telesales *Spiced With The Magic Of Neuro-Linguistic Programming*"

What does this mean?

This guidebook provides the tools and techniques of both telephone selling and some Neuro-Linguistic Programming (NLP) and will be useful primarily to people whose work involves selling over the phone, or where the telephone is used to follow up on field sales visits, and to close deals. (Not telephone marketing – lead generation and appointment making – see The Art of Telephone Marketing). For example:

Telesales Professionals   Who use the telephone as the primary tool for making sales.

Sales Professionals   Who use the telephone to manage their on-going sales leads, opportunities and accounts.

Anyone starting their own business   Who needs to learn how to build prospects and customers quickly through the skill of telephone selling.

Now, for those readers who like the big picture, the telephone selling structure takes the following format:

Attention:

- Introduction & Greeting
- Check convenience of the call (optional)
- Give reason for the call

Creating interest:

- Engage the prospects help
- Check roles and authority
- Skilful questioning techniques

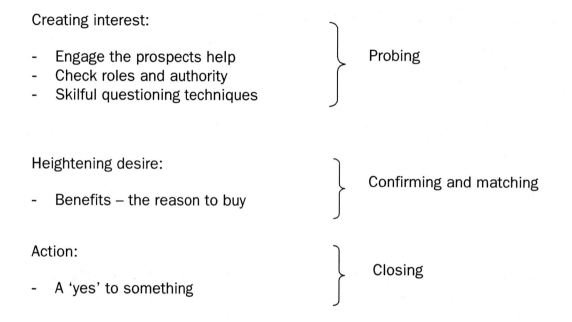

Probing

Heightening desire:

- Benefits – the reason to buy

Confirming and matching

Action:

- A 'yes' to something

Closing

The rest of this guidebook is the 'how to achieve all of the above' for those of you who like the detail and who want to learn the subtleties and the magical tips and techniques of this particular profession.

What is The Magic of NLP?

NLP is worthy of study if you want to be a peak performer and an excellent communicator. Superstar athletes all over the world understand the importance of practice and visualization. They can all be found picturing success in their minds before they perform, so their bodies follow through with what their minds have pictured. Whatever their challenge, they enter it first in their mind, get comfortable with it, and then do it. After each win, they are quickly back with their coach drumming through the basics and ironing out the wrinkles. [1]

For Telesales people it is exactly the same.

Whatever you think you are, you are so much more than that!

NLP offers you the tools for attainment of the highest business and personal goals.

So what is NLP?

NLP, an acronym for Neuro-Linguistic Programming, is the art and science of excellence. When we understand 'what makes us tick' and what strategies we run to achieve excellence, we can use the same strategies (ours or those of others) to achieve excellence in any area we choose to enhance.

How does NLP benefit your telesales world?

NLP:

- is one of the most powerful personal development tools available; (tools can optimise performance in any area of an individual's life – providing they want to change.)

- offers the tools to 'step into' somebody else's model of the world so that it is possible to understand and utilise their true motivation. Motivated people are highly resourceful people.

The ability for people to learn faster, communicate more effectively, and maintain high motivation towards personal and company goals may be the only sustainable competitive advantage as we hurtle through today's hectic business life.

It is generative learning. It is learning to learn, and creates continuous improvement, and self-fulfillment for you and others you encounter or empower.

For example, in any business situation it is critical to create rapport with those you meet. In all aspects of selling and particularly telephone selling this is a crucial skill needed to ensure the success of a sale. You cannot get any kind of agreement without rapport.

---

[1] "Principles of Peak Performers", based on research by Dr. Charles Garfield, Ph.D.

Perfecting The Art Of Telesales *Spiced With The Magic Of Neuro-Linguistic Programming*

Rapport is the process of responsiveness without necessarily liking. You may not like all the prospects you encounter and the customers you create as a result, but one thing is certain - you need rapport to have them buy from you.

Prospects will only buy people from people they like. People like people who are similar to them.

The powerful techniques of matching the other person's body language, pacing voice patterns etc., will create rapport instantly in a face-to-face situation – but what else do you need to do when dealing with people on the telephone to achieve the same level of rapport, i.e. as if you were like them, and with them?

When you gain rapport with other people, the lines to the telephone sales call flow open.

Rapport is one thing you do quite naturally but usually unconsciously, which means it is easy to be out of rapport, and not realise or know how to rebuild it.

This is one aspect this guidebook reviews, and together with other powerful techniques will accelerate your learning easily and comfortably. It will ensure you know how to gain and maintain rapport at will.

It gives you the greatest opportunity to be motivated to change, grow and succeed at telephone selling.

Why learn about NLP?

You may well have tried in the past to change your telesales techniques, and the methods you used did not seem to work and you reverted to old habits. This is because you have attempted change at a conscious level. All learning, change, behaviour is unconscious! NLP gives to you your unconscious key consciously; once understood, this allows you to change easily and effortlessly.

NLP techniques are based on powerful tools for change. The concepts and information embedded in this guidebook begin to uncover how you and your prospect use your minds during the telesales call.

I trust you will enjoy and benefit from this guidebook. Learn the basics then add the spice.

It is important that NLP is used with love and respect for yourself, your prospect and your customers. I request you, therefore, as students in this learning, to undertake to use the information and techniques only for the highest good of yourself and others.

I too, am serving you to the very best of my ability, with respect and integrity.

A smidgen about the beginnings of NLP

"How do we do what we do?" and "how could we do it better?" If you are already asking these questions then discovering NLP is a route to your answers.

Neuro-Linguistic Programming is based on the ideas of the anthropologist, Gregory Bateson, and was developed in the 1970's in California by a professor of linguistics John Grinder, and a mathematician Richard Bandler. They asked the question "what makes for excellence in the field of communication?" particularly in the area of personal development.

Through a process they developed, known as 'modeling', they observed what happened on various levels including linguistic structure (indicating thought patterns), language styles and physiology, comparing when things went well to when things went not so well.

They found that there were key patterns and variables in the processes, which went on whatever the content. These findings have been extended, refined, deepened and found to be extremely useful in a wide range of areas including psychotherapy, business, management, sales and education.

NLP is often defined as the study of "subjective experience", more colloquially it is finding out "how people tick". With it we can gain information at many different levels to create descriptions of everyday experience in terms of how we are perceiving, thinking and feeling. From this we can create new ideas and experiences and thus learn to manage much better how we do what we do. It also allows us to develop a greater understanding of how others perceive their world, thus vastly increasing people's potential for empathy, influence and opportunity to bring about growth and change.

The systematic approach of NLP strongly facilitates the learning curve of skill building, and telephone selling is an art and a skill. There used to be four stages of learning and now there are five.

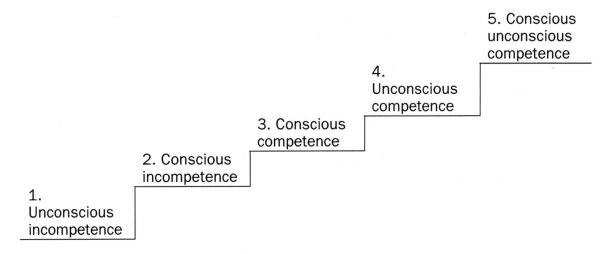

Perfecting The Art Of Telesales *Spiced With The Magic Of Neuro-Linguistic Programming*

I do not know where you are in your stage of learning; I can only guide you to strive towards stage 5, conscious unconscious competence. This will mean you will become fully conscious of what works well for you, and what does not, and therefore bring about appropriate change to improve. When your telephone selling becomes what you might call 'second nature' and it is working, as you would want i.e. you are truly aware of what works, you will have reached that level of being conscious of your unconscious competence.

In fact NLP is often referred to as the science of what works. Its building blocks have been developed not from theories, but from practical experience, and as such you can apply them to everyday life.

I have applied relevant NLP techniques as they complement telephone selling, hence the guidebook is primarily about the art of telephone selling and it is spiced with NLP.

What is selling?

Dictionary definition: -

1. To dispose of or transfer or be disposed have or transferred to a purchaser in exchange for money or other consideration. **2.** To deal in (objects, property, etc.) **3.** To give up or surrender for a price or reward: to sell one's honour. **4.** To promote or facilitate the sale of (objects, property, etc): publicity sells many products. **5.** To gain acceptance of: to sell an idea. **6.** To be in demand on the market.

However none of the above definitions describes precisely how much time, effort, energy and commitment goes into the process of selling in order to obtain the money, consideration, acceptance or reward.

This guidebook will provide the steps to help you obtain your chosen reward.

Why is selling really about buying?

No one is ever sold to; a prospect buys what he thinks a product/service will do for him.

1.   Sell the concepts - What the prospect thinks the product/service will do for him

2.   Sell the product   - Relate the product/service to the concept the prospect has

A sale is made when the prospect's need or desire to have/own your product/service is stronger than his natural instinct to hold onto his money.

It is your job to make the prospect aware of his needs and desires and help him make the decision to purchase your product/service.

What is Telephone Selling?

It is the means of contacting the maximum number of suitable prospects in the shortest time possible, and for the least cost.

It is the full selling process that is being completed over the telephone.

It cannot replace a field sales role where a product/service that due to its price or complexity has to be sold face to face.

If, therefore, you have a product or service that is of low value (meaning that the price of the product/service outweighs the cost of your making visits to sell it; or that it is a product/service that is easily recognisable for what it is; or you require volume sales on products/services that you have already sold) then using the telephone as the means to sell is usually very cost effective and profitable. Only you can be the judge of whether there is a marketplace for what you are selling.

The telephone is a major asset to any business, especially to anyone who knows how to use it efficiently and proactively, and answer it professionally.

The telephone is:

- Recognised as a very powerful instrument

- A medium used by virtually all businesses to communicate information quickly - it cannot be said effectively since there is a great deal of mis-communication in business (society) today

When you use the telephone for making or receiving calls you create an impression of yourself and the organisation in which you work or of your own business. Make it a positive, powerful impression!

A definition of the telephone selling process:

- Establishing and analyzing a prospect's **need** for your product/service.

- Getting him to acknowledge his need.

- Recommending the **product/service** that best satisfies that need.

- Persuading the prospect that the **source of supply** is satisfactory.

- Gaining his agreement that the **price is fair**, and now is the **time** to fulfil his need!

Perfecting The Art Of Telesales *Spiced With The Magic Of Neuro-Linguistic Programming*

Telephone selling is a two-way communication ending in the mutual satisfaction of both you and your prospect.

It is building the desire of the prospect on the other end of the telephone by convincing him that he needs what you are offering him, and that he is the one who makes the final decision.

Your 'offer' should always be relevant to your prospect.

Remember the purpose of all selling activity (whether telephone or field sales) is to direct the prospect's thoughts and preoccupation to your products/services. So:

- Settle the prospect into the right frame of mind in order to continue your sale

- Test your initial ideas about the decision maker, influencers, and his company

- Invite answers on which to build your case

- Add any relevant information to your knowledge about him

- Help to launch an exchange of ideas, and help him make up his mind to buy

- If you do not ask for the next decision, it has all been a waste of time

- Give the prospect something in return for his time and interest

- Give him information

- Whether he buys from you or not he has paid for your call in time

- Time is of great value to him

Other definitions to help you in using this guidebook:

Context
The dictionary definition says "The circumstances that are relevant to an event".

This particular word used in relation to the subject of NLP is to describe that changes in behaviour are also specific to an event, its time and place.

For example, you have different behaviours for shopping or going to the beach, being at a meeting in work, or at a party with good friends.

I have used this word many times in this guidebook, so I need to you consider that the 'context' I am focused on is telephone selling. Remember you will behave differently in other 'contexts' of your life.

Preference
The act of preferring.

The dictionary definition says 'Prefer' is "To like better or value more highly".

This particular word used in relation to the subject of NLP is to describe our 'unconscious' valuing heard in our language and seen in our behaviour.

Presupposition
The dictionary definition says "To take for granted".
"To require as a necessary prior condition".

This particular word used in relation to the subject of NLP is to describe 'convenient beliefs' not necessarily true, but when adopted, make the difference in achieving positive results.

The presuppositions of NLP **(see pp.128-131.)**

Part two

Traits of Successful Telesales People

Perfecting The Art Of Telesales *Spiced With The Magic Of Neuro- Linguistic Programming*

Remember - first impressions last!

Behind every sale are people - you and your prospect.

The USP (unique selling point) of any product or service is the telesales person involved.

Communicate an honest picture of yourself, your company and your products and services and not a favourable picture of how you want to appear.

You gain success by helping your prospect get what he wants, not what you want.

The selling purpose is about making your prospect feel good in himself and his decision to buy your product or service.

It is important for you to **believe** that you are going to succeed.

80% of your results are produced by 20% of what you do.

80% of your sales are produced from 20% of your customer base.

If 20% of what you do will give you your desired result, then let us concentrate throughout this guidebook on what that 20% comprises, starting with:

- Personal qualities

- Personality

- Effective communication skills

Personal qualities you need for successful telephone selling:

 **Imagination** – always look at your product/service from the point of view of your prospect – think and feel like him – see things his way.

 **Enthusiasm** – if you are genuinely excited about your product/service there is a good chance your prospect can be made to feel the same way. You need an abundance of high energy and a cheerful disposition to sell well.

 **Concentration** – your enthusiasm has to be focused and comes from having a defined goal at which you can direct your energy.

 **Persistence** – your prospect may be slower than you would like in his decision-making, and you may be tempted to give up too soon. If you want to excel at telephone selling keep focused. You will learn the value of persistence - it always pays.

 **Sincerity** – is an asset. If you say you are going to do something, do it. If you cannot or do not want to do something, don't say you will. Never let insincerity cloud your judgment or sunny disposition by misleading your prospect or by breaking a promise.

 **Memory** – A poor memory is a handicap. A good memory in telephone selling is very beneficial. Rather than rely on it totally, always take notes. Keep a comprehensive prospect/customer contact system.

Perfecting The Art Of Telesales *Spiced With The Magic Of Neuro-Linguistic Programming*

You need to be: -

An active and effective listener – really hearing what your prospect is saying will tell you a great deal about his desires needs and concerns. Actively listen to what he wants. Use verbal nods – make listening noises down the phone, interject with relevant comments. Say, "Yes I understand", or "That sounds very interesting Mr.."

Be confident, cheerful, courteous and honest. And always show integrity.

When telephone selling you need to be sure that you:

- Communicate to the right prospect

- Communicate at the right time

- Communicate the right message

- Think before you speak

- Actively listen when your prospect is speaking

In effective telephone communication you must be:

- Clearly heard and understood by your prospect

- Able to maintain his interest

- Able to convince him

- Able to motivate him

Perfecting The Art Of Telesales *Spiced With The Magic Of Neuro-Linguistic Programming*

Projecting your personality

Get yourself in the right mood for telephone selling and start promptly.

Thoughts (are habit forming), and beliefs are generated from thousands of experiences you have and, once formed, they tend to be self-reinforcing. So make sure you are giving yourself positive, powerful messages. Just decide to feel great. Now! This moment.

Tell yourself everyday "I am going to have a fun-filled, successful and happy day" make this statement or one like it, each and everyday.
You could add, "I have wonderful prospects and customers, who are always delighted to hear (and buy) from me".

My point is if you set yourself up for success and decide in advance what kind of prospects and customers you want to do business with, this will become your self-fulfilling prophecy. I.E. You will create exactly those types of customers for yourself, and you will have a successful day everyday – despite the little obstacles that may arise – and you will be in a positive mindset to deal with them easily.

Be positive, confident, and cheerful, it will make the prospect's and your day better.

When your prospect answers your call, listen to how he sounds.

- If he sounds distracted – check convenience to continue

- If he is not listening, or not in a receptive mood, there is little point in attempting to engage him in conversation

- Get his agreement to call back at another time that is convenient to him

- Get an agreed date and time and call back then

- Make sure you call when you said you would

- Does your voice indicate that you are

	OR	
Bored		Enthusiastic?
Tired		Alert?
Aggressive		Calm?
Unsure		Confident?

Your voice reflects your mood. His voice reflects his mood. So pay attention.

Smile

- Introduce yourself clearly

- Speak slowly and distinctly

- Maintain an even rate of speech

- Make your voice animated and interesting

- Be friendly

- Be brief where necessary

- Be interested to be interesting

- Keep control

Use your voice

To get across mood, feeling, meaning:

- Raise your voice to emphasize a point

- Lower your voice to gain closer attention, to give a phrase a deeper meaning

- Stress certain words, just as you might underline them in writing, e.g. "He was **delighted** with the results"

- Step-up the pace. For example, in relating a testimonial, speed up the telling to a climax. Then change pace

- Slow down the pace. Talk slower for emphasis, to give importance, to inspire confidence

- Pause. A pause can add drama and heighten anticipation and curiosity. It encourages the prospect to talk if you stop talking

- Use rising inflection. A rising inflection at the end of a sentence indicates a question, help or interest

- Use a falling inflection. A falling inflection at the end of sentence suggests positiveness, earnestness, and finality

- Build personal voice improvement by listening to your own voice

- Tape your calls and listen to yourself

Remember:

- It is what you say and more importantly how you say it that counts

The importance of voice matching in building rapport. (**see pp. 143-144.**)

Requirements for effective telephone communication

Effective communication is the process of sharing ideas and information with others, gaining understanding and ensuring the desired action is taken. Remember: The meaning of your communication is the effect you make and the response you provoke.

You must be:

1. Prompt
   If you promise to call a prospect at a given time do so.

2. Polite
   Common courtesy demands that you explain the situation to the prospect, preferably before, not after any delay. Always apologise and keep him informed.

3. Prepared
   When you are going to call a prospect have all your information ready.

4. Precise
   A longwinded argument never wins a sale. What your prospect is interested in are the facts. Present them to him in a sensible order.

5. Professional
   Your prospect is interested in his business, his profits, his challenges, and not your income, your concerns, your hobbies. A prospect will always appreciate a business-like call showing how he can benefit. When you have built a relationship you will be able to have more social interactions. It is all down to the level of rapport you create.

6. Practical
   Give your prospect what he needs. Do not run up an expensive solution for someone who cannot afford it. Give him practical ideas, and he will buy from a practical person.

7. Pleasant
   Remember to be the first one to smile, its contagious!

8. Positive
   Be positive in your approach, thinking, ideas and manner. Never beg for business. Sell him (enthusiastically) give him logical reasons for buying, based on his buying motives.

9. Patient
   Bear trials calmly - your prospect may take several contacts to convince. Keep calm - Keep calling. Always re-sell the ideas.

Perfecting The Art Of Telesales *Spiced With The Magic Of Neuro-Linguistic Programming*

Active Listening

You only have one chance to actively listen.

- Hearing is a physical process.

- Active listening is an intellectual process.

Active listening is in four stages:

1. Sensing

- Is the message heard?

- Can you repeat it?

2. Interpreting

- Are your meanings the same?

- Do you understand each other?

3. Evaluating

- What is your judgment?

- Do you agree or disagree?

4. Responding

- How do you feel?

- You adopt whatever action/inaction you decide on.

Ineffective listening leads to:	-	Comment taken out of context
	-	Judgments made before understanding
	-	Disregarding new ideas

| Which results in: | - | Misinterpreting instructions |
| | - | Jumping to wrong conclusions |

Perfecting The Art Of Telesales Spiced With The Magic Of Neuro-Linguistic Programming

What prevents you from listening?

Losing attention Are you easily distracted? Do you daydream?	You can listen several times faster than your prospect speaks. So you sometimes get bored, and your mind wanders to your own thoughts or other more interesting distractions around you.
Do you assume you understand, when you don't?	When your prospect gives you information you do not understand, your mind tunes into the bits you can grasp and you delete the rest, but you pretend to know what he is talking about!
Do you mentally criticise the prospect?	You start to disagree with your prospect, and you start to mentally argue or criticise what he is saying. You do not express it verbally, but he will pick up your doubts in your tonality. Your mind becomes closed to what he is saying.
Do you interrupt?	You are anxious to make your point, or ask another question. Or he says something that triggers another idea, and you stop listening and want to have your say.
Do you hear what you want to hear?	You so desperately want him to accept your product/service that you perceive there is a need, when there isn't one. You often listen to the general sense of what is being said, but overlook the significance of key words and phrases.
Do you focus too much on the facts?	You hear too many facts, and try to assimilate them, but fail to really comprehend the essential messages, which may be far more important.
Are you too silent?	You are so anxious not to interrupt, and you may have learnt in selling that silence is powerful. It is, but it must be used wisely. Listening is an active process, which does call for questioning at the appropriate time to seek clarification and information. Use verbal nods to indicate you are following his train of thought.

We spend 45% of our waking hours listening, yet few of us hear what is really being said, or realise that what the prospect said, may not be what he meant!

Active Listening is an art requiring:

- Discipline
- Concentration
- Practice, practice, practice

To become effective as an active listener you must control your intellect, emotions and behaviour.

Tips for active and effective listening:

Ineffective listener	**Effective active listener**

Listen only for the facts.	Listens for central theme and ideas. Clarifies reasons for beliefs and opinions.
Inadequate note taking - not enough or too much.	Has a flexible approach to note taking. Easily notes essential points of interest and matters for clarification.
Is easily distracted by own thoughts or outside influences.	Concentrates and actively participates in the conversation with prospect.
Shows no energy or enthusiasm.	Exhibits an active body state. Imagines eye contact. Uses attentive verbal nods and gestures even though prospect cannot see him.
Resists difficult situations.	Treats difficult situation as a learning. An interesting mental exercise. Ensures future preparation is improved.
Switches off if prospect sounds boring.	Focuses on context, even if prospect is dull. Guides the conversation to find prospect's hot button to increase enthusiasm.
Never uses verbal nods to acknowledge what the prospect is saying.	Uses verbal nods to advantage. Summarizes and paraphrases understanding to gain commitment along the way.
Prejudiced when prospect devalues product/service. Becomes defensive.	Objectively considers prospect's views. Values and resets prospect's beliefs based on real evidence. Demonstrates assertive behaviour.

Perfecting The Art Of Telesales *Spiced With The Magic Of Neuro-Linguistic Programming*

Actively listen:

- For the sensory based language so you can understand your prospect's preferred communication channel **(see pp. 145-158.)**

- For how he sounds

- What is his mood? This is reflected in his voice, the way he first answers your call, how he controls the conversation

- To the words and tonality he is using

- With your own feelings/intuition for rapport and to grasp what he really means

- With your mind's eye so you can visualise the total message

- With the whole of your mind for what the words convey, do they make sense, if not, question and clarify

- For your prospect's meaning, rather than what you think he means.

Active listening can help you to:

- Excel at telephone selling

- Learn

- Make better decisions

- Help others

- Gain co-operation from others

- Become a caring human being

It takes time to build your capacity to actively listen, and it starts with you.

Start today, now!

Be an active listener

Actively listen to what is being said/or not!

When in doubt – always ASK!

How to actively listen when telephone selling:

Look interested	Maintain an active body state. Act as if the prospect is sitting in front of you. Take notes from the beginning of the conversation.
Inquire with questions	Gather the facts - remember to ask 'open' questions. **(see pp. 39,42,43,80,81.)**
Stay on target	Stick to the point - remember your purpose – to have him buy from you. Listen for the central theme of what is being said - think ahead - wait for the complete message - don't prejudge or interrupt – avoid saying "yes but" - be patient.
Test your understanding (and his)	Ensure you really do understand what your prospect is saying. Restate to make sure "So what you are saying is...." Repeat what you hear, and take notes – translating what you hear in written form involves more than just listening to the words he is saying.
Evaluate the message	Identify his needs/purpose. Analyse what he says. Reasoning –generalizations - facts or assertions - voice: - tone, pitch, pace of delivery of information. You need to put yourself in his shoes. What is he really saying to you? Is what he is saying, really what he means? Question and clarify.
Neutralise your feelings	Stay calm - retain self-control - never get heated or emotional - keep an open mind.

Your prospect is a person who has moods, just like you.

He has personal problems that affect him, and many pressures in his work. As a result he does not always behave in a respectful and cheerful way, and you may have just caught him at the wrong moment.

He has behaviour that is not who he is! Learn to separate intention from behaviour. Never be put off; later or tomorrow his behaviour will be different.

However, it has usually left you in a negative frame of mind, shake off any unresourceful feelings before you make your next call, otherwise it may affect it.

Perfecting The Art Of Telesales *Spiced With The Magic Of Neuro-Linguistic Programming*

Telephone selling requires maintaining a positive mindset. So it is imperative that you understand that:

- Events (behaviour/situations) - generate thought - thought provokes emotion - emotion generates behaviour. **(see p. 137.)**

So when:

- You can't change an event - change your thoughts about it.   When you think differently - you experience differently.

You don't get in life what you want - you get what you choose think about communicate - and are motivated to bring into your reality.

The only behaviours you can influence are your own!

Your prospect has not done anything to you – you have chosen how to respond to what he said and his behaviour – it does not have to be a negative response; you can choose to think differently and positively, and therefore experience the outcome differently.

Be at cause not effect!

It is vital that you understand the principles of cause and effect. When you understand that if you believe, and work on the principle that you are the cause of everything that happens to you, then you will know that how you react to his rejection and rudeness is within your control.

If you act as if you are the cause of what is happening, you will then be in a position to influence the outcome.

If you believe you are at effect (worry/concern) then you will make excuses to yourself and end up in a fixed, unresourceful emotional state. This is not useful, as it will put you off making more calls.

Stephen Covey[2] said there are two states we can operate in, one of cause (influence) the other of effect (concern and worry).

In the circle of concern we worry about all the things, which we individually have no control over (e.g. world poverty, global warming, etc).

Whereas, within the circle of influence are all the things we can change – essentially our own behaviour. The only areas you are entirely certain of changing are the ones within **your** circle of influence.

---

[2] Stephen R Covey, Seven Habits of Highly Effective People. (Simon and Schuster Ltd, 1992)

Perfecting The Art Of Telesales *Spiced With The Magic Of Neuro-Linguistic Programming*

Prospects are responsible for their behaviour.

You are responsible for yours. You are also responsible for your emotional state. He hasn't done anything to you. It is how you are thinking about the situation, and how you are choosing to respond that brings about your emotional state.

Direct your energy more fruitfully, particularly for telephone selling

Ask yourself after a negative call:

"How could I think differently?

"What could I do differently in the next call?"

"How can I generate a positive outcome?"

Generate a positive response for yourself.

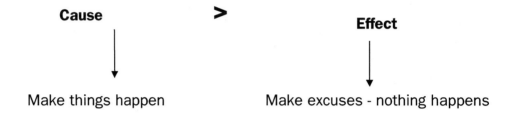

Cause > **Effect**

Make things happen   Make excuses - nothing happens

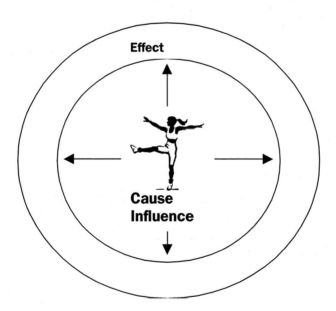

Focus on being at cause (influence) - the circle of influence will get bigger and concern (effect) smaller

Act as if.............you are the cause.

Note taking

Is an aid to active listening and it helps concentrate your mind. It is brain writing.

The purpose of note taking when on a telesales call is to use the information **during** your conversation with the prospect. It helps you to:

- Remember his name, and stops you making him repeat himself
- Clarify his needs
- Check understanding
- Test any contradictory statements
- Tag back information with the benefits of your product/service
- Demonstrate that you have been listening
- Prove that you understand what he has been saying to you
- Help you formulate your presentation, i.e. matching your product/service to his needs
- Helps you formulate a response using his style of language
- Remember the things he did not express interest in
- Remember the things he did express interest in

Note taking helps you detail and build your case for you to help him to make decisions to buy your products/services.

The purpose of notes **after** any telesales call is to record information that will help you progress your sale.

Keep comprehensive notes of your conversations.

Also make notes of:

- Questions to ask him next time
- Answers to objections that you could not answer this time
- Other details that will help you build a relationship with him
- Other prospects for your products/services
- Other products/services for this prospect

Part three

Preparation

Telesales planning & preparation

You should always have a framework in which your telephone sales techniques can be used effectively.

Planning encompasses many things to do with effective telephone selling. It is important to remember all of its aspects, not just one or two. Selling success is based on your:

	If you are employed by a company:	**Additional things to consider when you are in business for yourself:**
Business knowledge:	- Make sure you know in general something about your prospect's business - do research	- Be organized and ready - Be clear about how your business functions - Terms of business - Invoicing procedures - Cash collection (Cash flow is important to stay in business) - Remember, in your business - if you don't do it, it won't get done!
Product knowledge:	- You will be primarily working with the same products and services - Therefore you must be as familiar with them as well as the markets, industries, territories or sectors into which you are selling - As new products and services come on stream, learn about them	- Be clear about your products and services - what is it you are offering? - How does he buy from you? - What after-sales service do you provide? - What is your ongoing service? - What will you do if he is not happy with the product/service?

Perfecting The Art Of Telesales *Spiced With The Magic Of Neuro-Linguistic Programming*

Selling skills:	-	You may receive training and coaching if you are employed	-	You will be reliant upon developing yourself
	-	This guidebook will support you in self-development	-	This guidebook will help you build the skills needed
Company knowledge:	-	Familiarize yourself with your company's background and other products/services that may be available but not necessarily promoted by you	-	Think about your business history and credentials
	-	The company's history, market share, stability etc.	-	What your prospect may ask you about your background in relation to your product/service
			-	Have references ready
			-	Think about how you will prove what you have to offer
Industry knowledge:	-	Analyze the potential competition	-	Look at similar businesses to your own
			-	Who are they targeting?
			-	Where are they based?
			-	What do they offer?
			-	What can you do better?
			-	Do they pose a threat to your success?
			-	Do they pose an opportunity for your success?

- **You, and your positive mental attitude, and belief in yourself.**

- **Applies whether you work for an organization or for yourself.**

Telephone selling flow chart

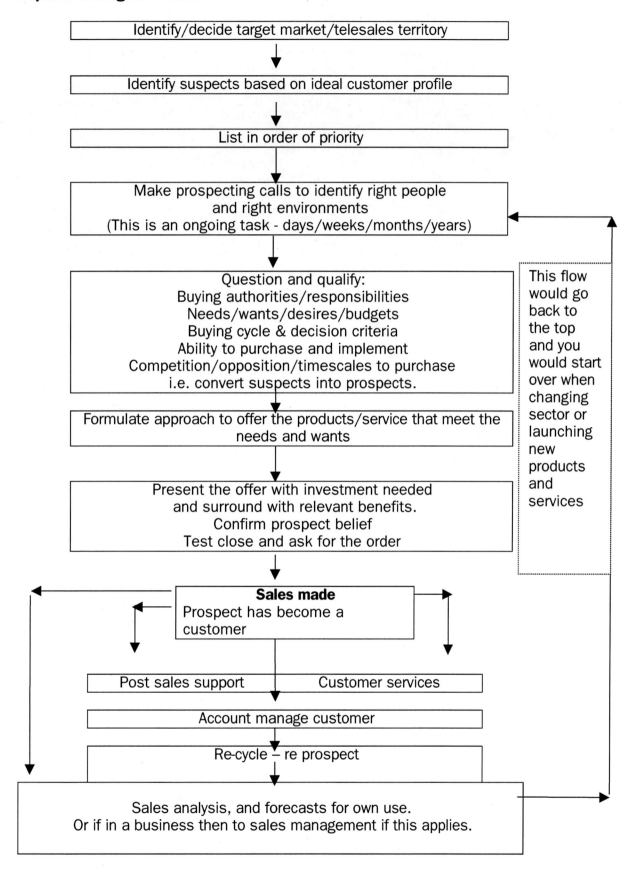

Perfecting The Art Of Telesales *Spiced With The Magic Of Neuro-Linguistic Programming*

Telephone selling cycle

Steps from planning call to happy customer!

1. Decide on industry/business sector, and establish ideal customer profile and sell to them.
    (This ideal profile means the sort of organization/person you would like to have as a customer; or shape and size organization that you have sold to before. i.e. companies where you will make profitable sales!) (An example is shown on the next page.)

2. Identify suspects based on ideal customer profile. (Suspects are those who you will convert into prospects; i.e. you 'suspect' you could do business with him but you have yet to qualify his real need/want that he has the money to spend and is motivated to do something to satisfy his need/want.)

3. Define and select the ideal accounts, and then gather knowledge of suspect's business.

4. Questioning and qualifying to: -
    a) Identify right people - decision-makers/influencers/buying process
    b) Analyze the needs of each level of authority
    c) Identify and define business problem/opportunity
    d) Identify (or anticipate) the decision-making process
    e) Identify opposition/competition

5. Qualify suspect in or out. (Qualification does not mean the suspect is a non starter; he may not be a prospect right now.) Those you qualify as potentials to do business with are now your prospects. (Prospects are those who have a need/want, the money to satisfy it, and the motivation to act to solve their problem or fulfil an opportunity.)

6. Determine your approach - the strategy. Find/create needs and turn them into wants. Formulate and propose product/service that will satisfy his needs.

7. Make follow-up calls to right people/right time.

8. When appropriate, and only if asked, send proposals or quotations. Never offer this as a matter of course. You may spend hours writing them and find the request was just an excuse to get you off the telephone.

9. Confirm prospect belief (testimonials or proof of concept).

10. Close business by obtaining an order. Organize product/service delivery and any other post-sales support.

11. Restart the cycle - account manage - find new opportunities within this new Customer; i.e. continue prospecting.

Perfecting The Art Of Telesales *Spiced With The Magic Of Neuro-Linguistic Programming*

Organize your contact lists and leads

Prospecting:

- Turning suspects into potential customers - prospects

- The search for potential buyers (these buyers maybe existing customers) is basic to all selling.

How to be a good prospector:

- It is not sufficient just to have a list of contacts.

- They must be qualified and screened.

- The ability to make a proper evaluation is important because time is wasted on chasing suspects that, for one reason or another, are unlikely to buy.

- The more information you have about your suspect the better your chances of success and turning him into a true prospect.

Who is the true prospect?

People may show a keen interest in your products/services, however, if they lack the authority to buy or make decisions or at least to influence, you won't get very far.

Large organizations are most complex. A director or senior manager may give you a sympathetic hearing, and may even show enthusiasm, but doesn't necessarily make the decisions.

It is, however, the best place to start. If he has delegated the authority, he will be reluctant to interfere. He will be able to steer you in the right direction.

The most senior person provides the permission to go on the hunt.

The hunt:

- To qualify if there are wants, needs, desires, plans that can be satisfied if he purchases your products/services.

You need to establish if your suspect has a need, a want, or plans where your product/service provides a solution to his problem or opportunity.

He may not recognize the need – so it is up to you to convince him.

What counts is your assessment of his situation.

Organize your contact lists and leads

Prospecting:

- Turning suspects into potential customers - prospects

- The search for potential buyers (these buyers maybe existing customers) is basic to all selling.

How to be a good prospector:

- It is not sufficient just to have a list of contacts.

- They must be qualified and screened.

- The ability to make a proper evaluation is important because time is wasted on chasing suspects that, for one reason or another, are unlikely to buy.

- The more information you have about your suspect the better your chances of success and turning him into a true prospect.

Who is the true prospect?

People may show a keen interest in your products/services, however, if they lack the authority to buy or make decisions or at least to influence, you won't get very far.

Large organizations are most complex. A director or senior manager may give you a sympathetic hearing, and may even show enthusiasm, but doesn't necessarily make the decisions.

It is, however, the best place to start. If he has delegated the authority, he will be reluctant to interfere. He will be able to steer you in the right direction.

The most senior person provides the permission to go on the hunt.

The hunt:

- To qualify if there are wants, needs, desires, plans that can be satisfied if he purchases your products/services.

You need to establish if your suspect has a need, a want, or plans where your product/service provides a solution to his problem or opportunity.

He may not recognize the need – so it is up to you to convince him.

What counts is your assessment of his situation.

If he has already bought more of your type of products/services than he can possibly use right now there is not much point in asking him to purchase more.

Find out what he does not have but would like or needs! Check also:

Can he afford to pay?

It is equally useless to sell on the need for your product/service and then discover he has no money, no budget, has cash flow problems or credit is bad.

Is the time right?

However much he may like what you are offering, he may be unwilling or unable to buy at this time. He may be going through tough times or the entire budget may be committed.

If you make your proposal at the wrong moment you are liable to get a negative response, regardless of the merits of your products/services.

You can of course gain an agreement to call back at a more suitable time, but the art of creative prospecting and telephone selling and the most effective use of your time makes it more sensible to concentrate on suspects that want to buy now because these are becoming true and immediate 'hot' prospects!

You are also beginning to create your *pipeline of opportunity - prospects that may buy later - and building relationships, which will enable you to call back at a later date to make a sale when conditions are more favourable.

You cannot win every sale every time; however, you must always end a conversation leaving the door open to go back.

Keep in contact on a regular basis - timing is usually determined by your prospect.

*A list of qualified prospects that have requirements, money and the motivation to act. (The timescale to the order will vary of course). This list of qualified prospects is known as being in your 'pipeline', i.e. opportunities to close business in the coming weeks/months. Pipeline building is crucial in all selling.

Priorities when prospecting

- List all the suspects you want to contact. Decide on those businesses you believe are the most vital to you ("ideal customers").

- Keep them in focus and don't waste time on those companies that have low potential or relatively small chance of being successful.

- Remember to appeal to the person's self-interest.

- Use language that appeals to the heart as well as the head - it is more attractive.

- However, remember it is hard to get an emotional response if he does not know what you are talking about! Go easy on the jargon.

- K.I.S.S. = keep it simple salesperson.

- Use language that he understands; business people talk and understand business matters - speak their language.

- Use positive words; never use words that create doubt in his mind, or words that imply you are unsure; 'later' or 'perhaps' are two such words.

- Avoid scare words like 'sign'. Most people hate to sign anything. Ask them to 'ok the paper work', or 'approve the form', and 'contract' implies a threat that if things go wrong he may end up in court.

- Avoid the word 'cost' - call it 'investment'.

- Your true prospect does not want to buy he (generally) wants to own. (This is not true for all products/services, since some products he can never own. Software products are an example where a customer sometimes pays for a license to use the product. Car leasing is another).

Personal preparation:

My mental state	
My emotional state	
My physical state	

"I am in charge of my mind therefore my results" – "Am I ready to make effective and successful telesales calls?"

"YES I AM!"

Work out a calling pattern:

- Plan out how many calls you may need to make, and how many presentations (actual meaningful conversations) in a day/week you will have to do that will enable you to make sales

- Check for callbacks that you have to make

Perfecting The Art Of Telesales *Spiced With The Magic Of Neuro-Linguistic Programming*

Make sure you have everything to hand - pens, pads, suspects and prospects lists and other leads and a quiet place with a working telephone.

Without effective planning you go into a telesales call in a weak position.

Planning simply consists of giving thought to your call before you make it.

Think:

Establish credibility.

Credibility is trustworthiness, believability and honesty.

It also involves having your prospect's best interests at heart.

If you do not have credibility with your prospect he will not pay attention to what you are saying.

You need to know your product/service.

Be able to explain your first hand experience and prove your track record.

Understand your prospect:

Who is he?

What does he already know?

What does he need to know?

What are his likely concerns?

What is at stake?

How much does it matter to him what you think?

What is the history?

Is there a poor relationship or service?

Is there an excellent relationship on which you can build?

Perfecting The Art Of Telesales *Spiced With The Magic Of Neuro-Linguistic Programming*

Just when you have finished thinking,   think some more!

What else do you think about?

Who am I calling?

Will it be a convenient time to speak with him now? (Consider his type of business. Some businesses have high activity periods during the year; e.g. it may be inappropriate to ring a chocolate manufacturer in the weeks before Easter or a brewery before Christmas).

Does he have authority, money and a need?

What do I already know about him or his company?

What has the previous relationship been?

Has he been a customer before, and why did he stop buying?

What are the needs of his type of business?

Who is his competition?

What do I need to find out about him?

What do I need to ask/tell him?

What do I need him to do?

What he likely thinks about?

Who is calling me and why?

Do I want to speak to him now?

Do I have the level of authority and enough money to spend on this product/service?

Have I heard of this company?

Have I ever done business with him before?

Do I want to discuss this now, or at all?

What needs do I have?

What is in it for me to act upon this request? Is this something my competition is doing?

Why should I answer his questions or listen to him?

Will his product/service satisfy any needs I have?

Am I convinced I should be involved?

Perfecting The Art Of Telesales *Spiced With The Magic Of Neuro-Linguistic Programming*

Why should he be motivated to do it?

What does my product/service do for him?

Who will benefit?
Will it improve my life/business in some way?

What is he likely to ask me?
What do I want to ask him?
When he buys my product/service will he be able to use it successfully?
Will he need other assistance?

What do I want to know about this company/product/person?
What do I need to know before I can make a decision?

What resistance am I likely to meet?
How will I handle it?

What will happen if I take action?
Am I interested in what he is offering/requesting?
Do I have to do this?
Do I want to do this?

What will happen if I achieve my outcome?
What will happen if I don't?

What will happen if I do take action?
What will happen if I don't take action?
What won't happen if I do take action?
What won't happen if I don't take action?

What is an acceptable alternative to my request/idea?
If there is one, how can I convince him of this?

What is an acceptable alternative to me?
Is it the right time for this kind of investment?

Then, **think** about:

- What are you going to say?
- How are you going to say it?

Your prospect is likely to be a purchaser of other products/services from an organization similar to your own – identify and examine the products/services they offer. Study the amount of promotion and advertising done by your competition.

Does your prospect's business have a lot of competition? Competitor activity could be one of the reasons he is in a 'buy mode', or you could convince him to be.

This gives you a better understanding of his business and ideas for converting him.

Make a list of the products/services that could be applicable for him.

Ensure all information and objectives are clearly defined.

Prepare a presentation remembering to ask for action that will achieve your objective.

Perfecting The Art Of Telesales *Spiced With The Magic Of Neuro-Linguistic Programming*

Keep your objectives in mind, which may be to:

- sell your products/services. (This objective is always to be kept in your mind);
- qualify real interest for future business;
- gather information about the prospect;
- give information;
- progress the sale;
- follow up on a lead;
- close the sale.

Realistically what can you achieve?

Prepare acceptable alternatives.

Decide what you want to achieve and then plan your activities to achieve it.

You are in the **'yes'** – getting business.

Decide what it is you want the prospect to say **'yes'** to! You are influencing your true prospect to make a decision in your favour.

When you have completed all your pre-call planning - you are in a better position to make your call.

When making your call, make sure your brain is in gear before opening your mouth!

Unsuccessful calls are generally the result of too little thinking and planning.

Think about:

- What you are doing.

- Why you are doing it.

- For whom you are doing it.

- How you are going to do it.

- When you are going to do it.

- Where you are doing it. (Are you in a comfortable place?)

- What if? Any other factors in relation to your product/service and calls?

- And remember if you don't do it, it won't get done!

Psychology of telephone selling

You have to learn to achieve and control the mental changes the prospect will make by understanding that he buys what he wants, so there is a two-step process:

1. To find out needs, wants, challenges or plans he has, is called finding the requirements (probing).

Probing means exploring needs and opinions by asking questions. It leads him to consider ways of solving his problem or fulfilling his opportunity. Use questions to confirm the product/service that will match his need. This technique gives structure to the call and gives him the feeling he is in control as the buyer.

Probing: Asking open and investigative questions

"What do you see as the key challenge you are facing?"
"What will it take for you to solve this problem?"
"What do you have now?"
"What do you like/dislike about what you have now?"
"What would you like to change?"
"Who else will be involved in this decision?"

Confirming: Asking closed and/or tie downs questions

"So what you are saying is this problem doesn't just affect your department?"

"If you were able to (state need) then you will be able to (state benefit he wants/or desired end result). Is this correct?

There are many other styles of questions you can use, which will be outlined later (see p. 42.)

This will also make your prospect feel that you are focusing on his real needs, and also ensures your recommendations will be tailored to meet them.

Questioning also allows you to listen, and you are learning what you need to know. Your job is to help him find the answers for himself, and then to focus on how you can help by providing him with your product/service – this is called the presentation part of the call.

2. Match what you are offering to his requirements (presentation).

Matching: Understanding the requirement, and making a judgement, and offering an appropriate and practical product/service.

"If I can show you a way to ...."

Closing: Gaining decisions in your favour so he purchases your products/services.

"To what extent would that be of interest?"

"What if you were also able to...?"

There is some additional information that complements the 'probing' aspect of the psychology of the sale. You need to understand:

1. The 9 stages of need

2. Styles of questions and their purpose.

1. The nine stages of need

1. Awareness of need	It is important to remember that your prospect tends to buy what he wants rather than what he needs. Both you and he need to be clear that there is a real need. The need cannot just be in your head. Sometimes he is too immersed in day-to-day operations to consider a better way of doing something. He may know there are improvements needed but not how to go about dealing with them. He may have tried changes before which didn't work, so he is reluctant to change.
2. Awareness of product or service	Your prospect wants to know that your product/service really exists; i.e. you are not selling 'futures'.
3. Knowledge of the product or service	Your prospect needs to be sure about the features and benefits of the product/service, how it will be used, the impact, the cost and so on. Until he has these facts he cannot proceed.

4. Is the product or service different?	Your prospect will make comparisons particularly with products/services he may already use. He may also look for differences, not necessarily the advantages, because unless it is different and improves his situation he may not bother to look any deeper. He may consider internal answers to the problem rather than go to an external supplier.
5. Is the product or service better?	Your prospect needs to see, hear, feel, sense there are differences, and that the product/service is better than that he is currently using; or he can see how he can do more, or more for less money or time; or it is better than doing nothing at all?
6. Commits to using product or service	When your prospect has gone through all the above thought processes, he will commit to trying out the product/service. It is at this point **he becomes a customer**. If he is the sort of prospect who knows what he wants and where he wants to go, he may also be challenged and excited by achieving what he wants... (this is the dream prospect). So he commits to a way forward.
7. Satisfy self	As the customer, he now has to satisfy himself that he has made a good decision; that the product/service satisfies his needs or compares favourably or better than the products/service he already uses (or has used); or is better than previous inactivity.
8. Wider usage of product or service	He will defend his decision having decided to buy the product or service. Once he has seen it as being different and better, he will use the product/service more widely, or more often. The more he uses the product/service, the less likely it is that product failures or service issues will influence his overall opinion of the product/service.
9. Incremental sales of the product or service	It is now that he is open to persuasion to expand the usage of the product/service into other areas or contexts. You have to remember that he needs suggestions - he will not find them on his own. Your job is to make him aware of the possibilities and opportunities that will reinforce and support his previous decision. Once he is a happy customer he will be willing to give you other names of people who you can also prospect. Ask him for referrals.

Perfecting The Art Of Telesales *Spiced With The Magic Of Neuro-Linguistic Programming*

2. *Styles of questions* ordinarily used in telephone selling to help you get your prospect to make an advantageous buying decision

Style of question	Purpose	Examples
Open and investigative questions	To encourage factual and truthful answers	How, what, why, when, where and who. (NB: 'why' should be used with caution as in telephone conversation it can make you sound overly aggressive and rude.)
Closed questions prompt yes/no answers.	To gain confirmation or clarification	Do, could, shall, can, if, will, are, and did.
Probing questions	To expand the conversation. Understand reasoning	"How would you go about doing this?" "In what way do you see this solving your problem/or realizing your opportunity?"
Evidence questions	To challenge ideas, seek proof	"How do you know this would work?" "What makes you think so?"
Questions of possibility	To offer new ideas (which may be less popular); or change the course of the conversation	"What would happen if you didn't do it this way?" "What wouldn't happen if you did?"
Contribution questions	To provide an idea of your own	"I have seen my product/service working for similar organizations, so is this a solution for you too?"

Perfecting The Art Of Telesales *Spiced With The Magic Of Neuro-Linguistic Programming*

Tie-down questions	To test the true response of your prospect to your suggestions. They encourage a commitment and decision about something, the answers to which encourage a decision in your favour based on a true fact/benefit about your product/service	"Wouldn't you agree that...?" "Isn't it true that?" Or you could end a statement with "You can see how that will work can't you?"
Alternative questions	To make a decision or gain agreement to options given	"Which of these dates are best for you X or Y?" "Which of the products offered so far is best for you X or Y?"
Direct Agreement questions	To gain an action	"We are agreed this is the next logical step then?" "Can we agree that you are going ahead then?"

The purpose of structured questions - to create interest.

What do you need to know about your prospect and his business? The facts!

The objective of thorough fact finding (effective questioning) is to:

- establish a business need or a desired end result;
- avoid unnecessary resistance and objections later in the call;
- arouse interest and establish what your prospect needs;
- structure questions because they are backbone of an effective successful call.

Thorough fact-finding is important as it influences not only this potential sale but also future sales.

Fact-finding must be conversational and not an interrogation.

By being and sounding enthusiastic, and showing interest, you will prompt your prospect to talk more.

Communication involves both talking and listening. Your prospect will warm to you if you allow and encourage him to talk. You actively listen, and take notes.

Structured questions help you to control the call and are designed to make the prospect provide information. It is imperative to find out the prospect's needs before selling him your product/service.

Never assume you understand the prospect's situation - it is important to find out the facts.

It is important to get a broad understanding of:

- the company's current business status;
- the challenges he faces in e.g. expanding, recruiting the right staff, etc;
- how he intends to make the business more efficient;
- how he intends to make the business more profitable and competitive, etc.

It is up to you to assess which of the prospect's challenges is most appropriate to pursue.

Where you find one opportunity remember **there may be more**. **Keep probing** across all areas of the business that he is concerned with, and where your product/service can be helpful.

Ask about the costs of what he is doing or intends to do. (This is how you build your case for him to spend money on your product/service.)

Ensure your product/service will be of benefit before making recommendations.

Once you understand that there is a psychology to telephone selling, and a purpose to structured questioning - it is imperative that you gain an equal understanding of buying and some of its characteristics.

Psychology of buying

Why do prospects buy?

Prospects buy from telesales people they like.

Rapport is one key to successful telephone selling; without rapport it is not possible to gain agreement.

To be effective and successful in telephone selling you have to know why prospects buy.

These are the mental steps that any prospect has to go through before he will make any purchase:

- Interest aroused

- Need, want, desire, requirement appreciated

- Knowledge of products/services extended

- Suitability appreciated

- Desire to buy

- Consideration of price

- Value appreciated

If any of these stages are missed then he will not buy!

Buying influences

Knowing what influences your prospect, how he feels about you, how he feels about your product/service, what questions he needs answered, how your competition is placed and a host of other things, helps you understand your current position in relation to him.

Different people in organizations see things in different ways, so where you have more than one decision-maker for the same product/service, they will all have different reasons for buying. You need to understand what will motivate each of them.

1. Prospects are not neutral

2. They buy needs and wants

3. They buy benefits not features

4. Decision-makers and influencers see benefits in different ways.

Different types of need:

Prospects buy to satisfy needs, which may be

-   Conscious
-   Subconscious
-   Practical
-   Emotional

Prospects prioritize their spending, and as the telesales person you aim to take care of fears, pain, essential and urgent needs, wants, before fulfilling goals and dreams.

Determine priorities and adapt your approach accordingly because people have different motives for buying.

So, in order to understand your prospect, his needs and wants, you have to be clear about who you want your ideal and true prospect to be and what makes him buy. He needs to feel confident in you, your company and it's product/services.

Remember:

You may also have more than one prospect in the same organization buying different products/services. This means you have to appeal to their respective needs. Each of them will perceive the benefits in different ways based on how they feel about their own requirements, and their status in that company.

It is important:

- To know your prospect's roles and responsibilities. People love to talk about themselves, so ask.

- To create the right structure, to approach the right people, about the right thing, at the right time

To understand the buying process

1. Level of authorization:
   - What is needed to make the sale happen?
   - From whom exactly must the authorization be gained?

2. Approval routes – what is the process for purchase?

3. Administration procedures – what process, if any, must be followed? e.g. a purchase order number must always be given to suppliers; no work should be undertaken and no invoice can be paid without it.

4. Any internal political factors – people in organizations have political agendas.

   On a telesales call these types of issues are rarely encountered; however, if you do meet with a 'politically-minded' prospect then it is likely you are talking with the wrong person. This is the reason we start high up in the organization and work our way down is to avoid 'treading on someone's toes', metaphorically speaking. The top-down approach means we learn about who has the real power as opposed to those who perceive they have it!

5. Any unresolved technical considerations – if the prospect has a similar product or experience of a similar service to your own, which has not worked well, then this may raise questions about the viability of your product/service. It is better that you find this out early in the conversation so you can be prepared to handle any concerns.

Buying decisions in organizations

An organization buys products/services because they meet the needs of the company, or the needs of an individual.

Buying criteria:

-   Product/service - features and specifications
-   Meets the need – i.e. fit for purpose, suitability for the operation/application
-   Source of supply – quality of product/brand name
-   Cost – value appreciated
-   Delivery time – within timeframe required by the prospect

A large organization will also consider the broader issues, and these matters raise questions in a prospect's mind. I would say that for most products/services sold over the telephone they will not generate this level of query, but it is useful to be aware of them should you move to face-to-face selling of high value products. The issues are:

1. Financial
    -   How will buying this product/service affect the balance sheet?
    -   Will manpower be required? Will the cost of labour increase?
    -   If we pay up front will we get a discount?
    -   Can other payment terms be arranged?

2. Macro-economic
    -   What is the cost of borrowing? Are interest rates likely to rise or fall?
    -   Is it the right time for a major investment?
    -   Should we wait for signs of economic recovery?

3. Technical
    -   Does it meet our specification?
    -   How does the product/service rate technically?
    -   Will the product be obsolete in a few years?

4. Environmental
    -   What impact will this product have on the environment?
    -   What is the likely effect on the public and our workforce?

5. Corporate or personal
    -   Unsure about role or judgement
    -   Uncertain how colleagues will view decision
    -   Afraid product/service will make job harder in some way
    -   Afraid product/service will make him or company appear technically incompetent, or that it will undermine the company or his role in some way

All these pressures affect the behaviour of your prospect, which shows how differently people are influenced and make decisions based on their model of their world.

If any stages are missed, objections could be raised, and these will be based on any one of those buying decisions or a combination of them.

Buying motives

Business (any business) is about creating profitable customers.

When a business is a 'going concern' it has organized its suppliers, staff, capital etc. To keep going at even the same size, it has certain business needs; to expand, it has other needs.

Business needs are the reason for which your prospect buys, and his overall attitude to corporate business efficiency and profitability.

Remember, when someone reaches the stage of wanting to buy for motives, he then justifies his wanting to buy, for a reason.

Why do business people buy? For these reasons:

- Profit (anything that increases it)

- Prestige (anything that enhances it)

- Continuity of the business (anything that will help ensure it)

- And because of their competition (anything that will help them beat it)

Examples of business buying motives

Profit buying motives:

- Increase new business
- Increase overall volume of business
- Secure new customers
- Attract quality customers
- Attract customers by price
- Attract customers from other locations
- Attract cash customers
- Attract quantity customers
- Draw customers from poor market locations
- Develop enquiries for the sales force
- Increase sales of certain products/services
- Increase business during certain hours
- Increase personal profit share
- Increase salary and bonus
- Increase productivity
- Increase efficiency

Prestige buying motives:

- Attract quality customers
- Increase prestige and improve public relations
- Overcome previous bad reputation
- Increase personal profile within the company
- Increase likelihood of a promotion
- Increase likelihood of getting a better job elsewhere

Competition buying motives:

- Overcome competitors' activities
- Attract customers by price
- Attract customers from certain locations
- Draw customers from poor market locations
- Appeal to specialized markets
- Increase the sales of certain products/services

Continuity buying motives:

- Avoid losing existing customers
- Avoid job losses
- Likelihood of promotion within same organization
- Remind customers of all lines of products/services offered
- Build up service business
- Line up business in slack periods

Prospects make emotional purchases for logical reasons:

-	Gain of money	Saving of money - something for nothing
-	Caution	Fear - if he doesn't do it now he may never do it
-	Utility value	Something that enables life to go along smoothly
-	Pride	To satisfy pride, something to talk about
-	Sentiment	For comfort
-	Pleasure	To rest, enjoy
-	Benefits to health	The world has become health conscious

Prospects also have personal buying motives, for example:

- Ego, status, security, satisfaction

- Comfort, convenience

- Increases his personal knowledge and experience

- Improves his image in the company

- Increases his profit share

- New information keeps him updated – ahead of the game

Buying decisions

It is not sufficient to understand the prospect's buying motives. It is critical to know his buying decisions. If any of the stages of the transaction are missed he will not buy, and his objection will be based on a buying decision or a combination of them:

- **Need:**

   The prospect must have specific needs. Agreement must be reached that your products/services will satisfy that need.

- **Product:**

   Agreement (in this case it will be verbal) must be reached that your product/service will satisfy his business and/or personal need. Sometimes it is an unspoken agreement, for example when he is already using a similar product/service.

- **You** (does he like you?) (Can you answer his "prove it" request):

   Can the quality of your products/services be proved? Third-party proof (i.e. people who have already used and benefited from your products/services and are willing to act as a testimonial.)

- Source of supply:

Any objections he may raise can be handled with direct benefits of owning your product/service, and that these benefits can be directly obtained from this one source, meaning you and your company. The prospect must be made to want to buy enough to outweigh any prejudice.

- Time to buy:

Now!
You have reached the stage where you can recommend your product/service you should be able to close the sale. So, providing your are talking to a decision- maker, and you have created enough urgency, and desire during the conversation it is time to get a 'yes' - a decision now. Do not allow him to 'cool off'.

- Price:

The prospect must agree that your price is acceptable (value for money). This may mean he can appreciate that when he uses your products/services they compare favourably with other products/services he uses.

Possible buyer behaviour

Your Prospect   **You**

When you make a call you will receive a variety of responses and here are the things you need to consider as to the reasons why, and what you can do about them.

A Manager in an organization is a 'very expensive' busy person. The more senior he is the more expensive and therefore the more reluctant he will be to talk to telesales people. In general he does not regard talking to you as part of his job. Nor is he sitting there waiting for you to call him today.

He is likely to be thinking about something else when you call.

He may be, and may sound, distracted; for example you can hear him talking to someone else as he picks up the phone.

Be sensitive and considerate of him and his time.

Check if it is convenient to talk.

Now my view about checking convenience:

As a rule because business people receive so many telesales calls, when you get him on the phone you will want to have a conversation. You have to make a judgement about whether it is going to serve you to check convenience or not, because it will be easy for him to say, "no it is not", and you have lost your opportunity.

My personal view is this: I always work on the principle that if he picks up the phone he has already made a decision to have a conversation with me. I am an equal. My time and money is just as valuable and important as his. However, it is critical to get to the point, to engage emotion quickly and of course this happens through planning your call, sounding authoritative and saying something relevant and intelligent.

However, there are also times when you just 'know' now is not the right time. Trust your instinct, and ask if it is convenient. He will appreciate that you are considerate of his situation and time. This consideration puts you up in his estimation and sets you apart from others who call.

Perfecting The Art Of Telesales *Spiced With The Magic Of Neuro-Linguistic Programming*

If it is not convenient to talk now, make an arrangement to call back – get a telephone appointment – date and time and call back. You cannot make a presentation to someone who is not listening.

The first impression you make when you start your call, and the way you leave any of these conversations contributes to the success of your sale.

However, it has also been my experience that the higher up the organization you call into, the easier it is to gain a hearing. Directors and senior managers may be very expensive busy people but they are also the people who need to know about products and services that will make their company more profitable, competitive, stable, or enhance its image.

These people know where they have (or think they have) delegated authority to, and will point you in the right direction, i.e. tell you whom to speak to about your offering. When you move top down in an organization the next level of managers will take your call because you have been speaking to the boss or someone more senior than they.

The lower down the organization you make calls into, the harder it becomes to gain attention and interest. Moving up the organization is a lot harder - not impossible, but it makes for a slower sales process.

Middle managers are immersed in day-to-day problems so spend less time considering new and better ways of doing things, and are even more reluctant to take your call. This group of prospects is likely those who say, "I am not interested".

This 'not interested' response may simply mean:

He cannot talk to you right this minute because it is not a convenient time to talk, but he does not say all this – he says, "I am not interested".

It is not his decision but he hasn't time to explain this to you, and you did not ask him – he says, "I am not interested".

He cannot talk to you as he is in the middle of an interview/meeting and he should have diverted his calls but forgot, and hasn't time to say this, and will look stupid if he does – he says, "I am not interested".

It could mean you are the fifth person who has called him this morning and you sound just like everyone else he has spoken to, and he just doesn't want to listen – he says, "I am not interested".

There are endless reasons, as you can see, why you may receive such a response, which is why your introduction must be creative, imaginative, stimulating and interesting.

The **mental processes** your prospect may go through:

Attention

Prospect: "Why does the telesales person want to talk to me?"

You: Be clear in the purpose of your call.
Prospects have short attention spans – engage his emotion quickly. Ask relevant 'open' questions.

Speak business language and establish that the prospect has a need, problem or opportunity that is current, significant and solvable.

Interest

Prospect: "What do you want me to do about it?"

You: Briefly describe the solution you are offering.
Show the probable positive effects on the business of his purchasing your products/services.

Desire

Prospect: "How will I know it will work?"

You: Establish credibility through hard evidence, and testimonials

Action

Prospect: "What is the next step?"

You: Agree the decision-making process and action plan.

The structure and application of A I D A will be explained later (see pp. 63-68.)

Part four

Telephone Selling

Perfecting The Art Of Telesales *Spiced With The Magic Of Neuro- Linguistic Programming*

The telephone selling process

Telephone selling and communication is the process of sharing information and ideas with others, ensuring understanding and getting the action you desired - a sale!

You cannot take anything for granted.

Telephone communication requires taking information from inside the prospect's head and converting into something that can be recognized as the real need by both you and he.
Both pieces of the sales jigsaw must fit.

 You have to create mental pictures, or give him a feel for what it is; to make it sound interesting, or have him talk about what sense it makes to have or own your product/service.

Remember, selling is about buying. It is persuading the prospect that he needs what you are offering, and that he is the one who makes the final decision to buy.

Teleselling is not just a warm smile, smooth tongue, friendly telephone manner, or good luck. Nor is it a battle of wits.

Teleselling is using knowledge to help your prospect understand his needs and solve his challenges with the benefits of your products/services.

Remember:

-   The end of the sale to you is only the beginning of the purchase for your new customer!

-   Not every prospect becomes a customer - for a variety of reasons: even when you have done a stunning teleselling job - he may not buy. You cannot win a sale every time!

Qualification – a critical and an iterative sales task

True prospects have to fulfil certain qualifying criteria before we can help them to decide to purchase.

Why? Because responding to a prospect's need absorbs an enormous amount of resource (people, money and time). In this case it is your time and money.

You need to ensure that you respond only where a conscious and objective decision has been made regarding the probable return expected from your investment, i.e. the cost of sale.

The qualification is an iterative process: until you find out about the decision-maker, influencers, the details of business needs, opportunities, budgets, existing solutions, his environment, buying process, and where the company plans to go in the future, there will be no point in your making a response.

Only by understanding how you can assist him in meeting his goals and fulfilling his dreams will you be able to provide a product/service in which he will want to invest.

This qualification process will narrow the number of possible suspects into 'true' and/or 'hot' prospects for which you can actually tailor your product/service. You will then be in a position to present it to the true prospect in his own language and create a win/win situation.

You must examine closely the prospect's business needs, which can be:

Actual	+	Future
Admitted	+	Hidden
Known	+	Ignored
Distributive	+	Total needs

These various needs create your pipeline of opportunity. Needs now, and those needs still to be admitted and understood that form hidden or ignored needs, i.e. not immediate needs.

You have to establish if your prospect has a real business need/opportunity, want, desire or plan where your product/service provides a solution. He may not recognize the need – you have to convince him, and create a sense of urgency to help speed up the buying process and decision-making.

Asking questions early in the telesales process will enable the information to become available to make objective decisions about all of these factors, which influence the success, and the speed of your sale.

During **qualification** you have to be able to answer **two questions**:

1. How serious is the prospect about doing business?

2. How attractive is this opportunity to you and your organization?

The degree to which you can answer these questions indicates how well you have qualified the opportunity to sell.

Because you will need to qualify:

- Out prospects that cannot buy from you at all
- Your true prospects, and establish those who are able to buy from you now
- Those you need to keep in touch with, i.e. prospects that have needs, but not now

There are mnemonics to help you remember and prompt the qualification questions. One is M.A.N.D.A.C.T = the qualifying criteria of every telesales call. This mnemonic will help you to remember to keep checking and rechecking information at every stage of your sale.

It is used to prompt answers to questions as early as possible in the telesales process and enable information to be available to make an objective decision about the value of proceeding with the opportunities presented.

Influencers are not direct decision makers although they may be an important and integral part of the buying process, and you always have to know what level of prospect you are dealing with, and what decisions, if any, he can make.

Money	Who has it? Is there money budgeted for this requirement?
Authority	Who has authority to spend the money? Whose support and decision is also required?
Need	Is the **MAN** with the money also the one with the business need? If not, who has the need? Is this business need or problem a priority for management? If it isn't, you may find it a challenge to gain a decision

Note: In complex sales, meaning where there is more than one decision maker in the buying cycle, money and need are commonly, but not always, at different levels within the organization. In general, products and services that are sold over the telephone are unlikely to be of such high value that there will be more than one decision maker, although there maybe several influencers.

Decision Criteria	What are the factors he will consider in choosing a supplier? How well does your company, its product/service match them?
Ability	Are there resources available on his side to implement or organize the use of your product/service? If not, do you have the capability and/or the resources to help him?
Competition	What is the involvement of your competition? What is the opposition? (People in his company who resist change and those who have purchased similar products/services and have other preferred suppliers)
Timing	What are his timescales to solve his problem/meet his challenge? Can you meet his timescale?

Remember too, *you* have a choice.

As a supplier you can also choose not to do business with a particular company or prospect. Where the qualification criteria cannot be satisfied, you will either need to keep probing until it can, or qualify yourself out from this particular opportunity.

If at any stage you realize that you cannot fulfil the request then, have the confidence and courage to walk away from this particular opportunity. Honesty with your prospect and with yourself saves time and effort. Prospects respect telesales people who recognize that they may not be able to help this time. Walking away this time can bring more business in the future. You will have built trust and integrity with your prospect.

Make a list of your own relevant qualification questions

Money	
Authority	
Need	
Decision criteria	
Ability	
Competition	
Timing	

Perfecting The Art Of Telesales *Spiced With The Magic Of Neuro-Linguistic Programming*

A.I.D.A. is a mnemonic to help you remember the telephone conversation structure

Attention

Greeting, introduction, reason for the call, and qualification of the buying authority

Interest

The purpose of questioning is to bring your prospect into the conversation and find out his desires and needs
Establish needs by asking have or want questions
Create and maintain interest by using open-ended questions
Use MANDACT questions/qualification
Listen actively and take notes

Desire

Appeal to the prospect's self interest
Be sincere and use positive powerful words; positive words trigger the right emotional responses
Summarize your understanding of his requirement
Give **relevant** benefits in relation to **specific need** and **gain agreement** of each
Mention past successes establishing you have a good track record, and use testimonials. Anything that takes the sting out of him parting with his money improves your chances of gaining your sale
Tell him how you, or your company can help
He is buying your desire to help him, so show, tell, give him a sense or feel of how you will help
Use tie down and test close questions

Action

Closing the sale. Get a '**yes**' to something
Ask the closing question – gain your sale
Or gain a decision in your favour
Agreement to a next call

A reminder:

Your presentation must be clearly understood by your prospect

It is hard to get an emotional response if he doesn't know what you are talking about. Go easy on the jargon. He understands and talks business language. Use language that appeals to his heart as well as his head - it is more attractive.

Perfecting The Art Of Telesales *Spiced With The Magic Of Neuro-Linguistic Programming*

Other components of the call structure

Attention

- Introduction/check convenience (when appropriate)
- Deal with reception/secretaries (in fact anyone who answers your call) with respect
  Be pleasant, friendly, and ask for their help. If you are offhand, pushy or rude they will prevent you from speaking to the prospect
- Opening the conversation
- Give a solid and interesting reason for your call

Interest

Establishment of needs, wants, desires and your main objectives are:

- To find out your prospect's personal, business needs, wants, desires, challenges and plans. (Planning in business is not concerned with future decisions but with the future impact of present decisions)

- Qualification of the buying process: this means 'who' the buying authorities are, the decision makers and influencers, and 'how' they buy

- Creating interest and establishing needs are achieved through effective questioning which means asking for information (fact finding) for example:

  - What he does, what he sells, what product/services, brands, what ranges, after sales services etc
  - What things concern him as an individual, or his staff in doing their jobs effectively
  - How he gains his business in his known markets and what he will do to develop his unknown markets
  - What areas he covers - where his customers are at present and where he would like them to be
  - To whom he sells - domestic, commercial, industrial
  - Special features - reliability, guarantees, competitive prices
  - Costs he incurs running the business - how many people employed, suppliers, sorting out legal situations, how he keeps himself updated on relevant business information etc
  - Trading areas - establish whether your prospect is likely to stay in the home market or sell in the rest of world

You will need to ask relevant questions in relation to whatever product/service you want him to buy. Use MANDACT to help you cover all the sales/buying bases.

Desire

Presentation of your products/services

The main objectives are:

- To sell the power of using your products/services
- To explain what your products/services mean to him
- To enable you to be able to prove the value of his using your products/services
- To give him a brief but comprehensive idea of the features of your products/services linked to benefits - what is in it for him to buy from you?

See his market, concerns, wishes, needs first and your products/services second. Remember, he is only interested in what they will do for him.

In other words, how it will work for him?

The main objective is showing him how your products/services will work to bring him the things he wants, and satisfy the personal and business needs you have established with him.

You need to show him how your product/service will work to bring him a more profitable business, and/or personal and financial success.

His concerns are, and will continue to be:

1. Establishing and maintaining his known market.

2. Tapping into his unknown market. Consider: establishing a business costs a lot of time and money in advertising, employing staff, getting suppliers, premises, etc. His business expands by tapping into unknown markets, and by maintaining the company's position in his established markets.

Your prospect has to maximize on his personal as well as his business investment and he knows that in order to continue to be financially successful, he must make certain that all existing and known sources of business information, efficiency, productivity, etc. continue to be under constant scrutiny and review.

He must also ensure that he is constantly kept aware of what is new and useful in the marketplace to make his company more profitable. This may well be your product/service.

Remember:

- It is the value and cost of the products/services you sell versus the things he has already done, will need to continue to do, and how much it costs to achieve them, that you are trying to establish

- Once you can show that the cost benefit of your product/service is far lower than is current expenditure, and/or it will help increase efficiency and productivity and therefore profits, he can be persuaded

Your recommendations:

- Having stimulated the prospect's desire to buy your products/services you go on to recommend those that best suit his business/personal needs

- The objective of the sales presentation is to find out what your prospect needs or wants and to match it

- If you ask for the order before the matching is complete he will raise objections

- Consequently, prior to closing, you should test the matching by asking a test close question

- A test close question is any question, the answer to which confirms he has bought your product/service, or has bought your ideas so far

- When it is obvious from the test close question that he has bought, you move into the closing question

Action

Closing

Remember the following points:

- Seek buying decisions

- Commit

- Listen for buying signals

- Ask for the order

- Never be afraid of the prospect saying no!

The rules of closing:

- Never wait to be asked to quote the price

- Convert it into small units or relative terms - relate it to the safeness of using your products/services

- Quote price and sandwich between the benefits

- Present a tailored offer specific to his needs, and then he has no comparison

- Increase the price and sell him better value

A note: During the telephone selling process there are a number of conditions that must be fulfilled before a sale can be closed:

1   You must have attracted his attention, stimulated his interest, heightened his curiosity, and promoted his desire to buy

2   You must have established points of agreement throughout the sale

3   He must have a full understanding of what you are selling

4   He must trust you: have confidence in your product/service

5   You must close in the right way at the right time, by asking a closing question, which is any question the answer to which confirms he has bought (or bought into the idea so far)
    Whenever you ask a closing question keep quiet. The person who speaks first loses. If you stay quiet only two things happen, he agrees with you and buys, or he doesn't and he has an objection

6   You must prepare for a final 'no', which does not always indicate that he is not prepared to buy

To help you now to get from Attention to Action the rest of this section is devoted to the structure of the telesales call.

The telesales call

Getting through to your prospect

Firstly, you will appreciate that there are many people calling into the prospects you want to sell to. This creates an interesting challenge, and it is where your creativity comes into play. Think of clever, but not devious, ways of making contact with the prospect.

Secondly, there is an ever-increasing utilisation of voice-mail, and this is often considered by sales people to be a screening device to prevent them from making contact.

So, whilst getting through is more of a challenge these days, it is fun to think up new and inventive ways to get to speak to the prospect, and here are a few ideas that will help you:

- Call early, i.e. before the reception or secretary start work. Senior people in companies are often at their desks at 0800 hours or earlier!

- Call late, i.e. after everyone else has gone home

- Call into Accounts or other departments where calls are not screened before they are put through, and ask to be transferred

- Call into Sales, and ask for their help. Sales people can be sympathetic to your cause - they experience the same challenges!

Many companies have a 'no name' rule, i.e. they will not give out names of individuals.   There are several reasons for this:

1. There is constant turnover of the personnel through re-organisations making it difficult for them to keep their own information up to date...sounds ludicrous but it happens in large corporations

2. They receive many telesales calls and reception staff get bored with repeating the information

3. They want to avoid 'search and selection' companies seeking out their valuable staff and offering lucrative jobs elsewhere

- Call and ask for the department you want, and when you connect to a person's voice-mail, **pay attention** and **listen actively** *for the **name of the person*** you have reached. Now you have a name, you can call back and ask for them - this will help you overcome the 'no name rule'

Perfecting The Art Of Telesales *Spiced With The Magic Of Neuro-Linguistic Programming*

To overcome these challenges, you can also seek information from:

-   Annual reports – this has the senior management details and other beneficial information

-   Check on the company's website; it often lists the Board of Directors and Senior Management people. It often also has the latest press releases with quotes from individuals within the company, usually mentioned by name

-   Obtain, if you can a copy of the company's communication/product/sales brochures; these too have information about individuals

-   Company information is recorded at Companies House. The directors information is a matter of public record

-   Go to business libraries and look up company information

-   Read the trade press, articles and case studies about companies; people are often making quotes about their new products, mergers, takeovers, any success (or not) the business is experiencing

-   Read business newspapers; check out who are the 'movers and shakers' - big companies love to see themselves in the press; there will be pictures, quotes people's names and job titles more often than not listed with the article

-   Read job advertisements these provide many clues about an organisation; they give a lot of information about the company's success, growth and the improvements needed

-   Make friends with Reception and anyone in the organisation you get to speak with - most people are helpful if you treat them well; ask for direct line numbers if you cannot get names, or extension numbers which are often, but not always, the extension of the main number.

Be creative. I once set an exercise to a group of sales people I was training in Hong Kong. They had told me it was difficult to find new prospects because there were no company lists to be bought. I asked them to bring in copies of the 'South China Post' morning newspaper and we spent 15 minutes scanning it, and jointly came up with 48 suspects! There were companies who had won awards for best customer services, or who were reducing their workforce for this, that and the other reason; there were new director appointments, new contracts won or contracts lost all of this is business news, with the company name and usually with a quote from a 'named' someone from the company.

For example: The bank that had won an award for customer service was on the front page, with photograph of named person receiving the award. This meant we could call to congratulate him, and ask how he was going to maintain this position. It also gave us the opportunity to call all the banks that had not won the award to ask what they were going to do to ensure they did next time. Get the idea?

My point is, what is success to one company, may mean the need to achieve for another. The clues to good contacts are everywhere if you but look, so start looking.

The most important thing to say, however, is **never lie** about who you are and why you are calling. Never say it's a personal call in order to gain access to your prospect. Honesty always pays. Patience and perseverance will too.

Having reached your prospect, remember the aim is not to get him to make a hasty decision, but to have an intelligent conversation, where opportunities are explored to find common ground for a business relationship to be established. This way both of you will be winners!

Get to the point. Busy people have short attention spans. Engage his emotions. Prepare an effective intelligent and interesting 'attention generator'.

This means you will have to spend time researching more about your prospect's company and situations, e.g.: newspaper articles, contracts his company has won, advertising and any exciting or current news about his organization. This will get his attention.

He will love to hear about his company, its achievements; he will love to talk about himself even more!

Remember your first task is to arouse interest; he is not sitting there waiting for your call.

Project confidence and authority.

You are his equal.

Never be discouraged by rudeness; it isn't personal, and you haven't done him any harm. Just say "I am sorry I disturbed you, when may I call you back?" Get a date and time. "Thank you, Mr... I look forward to speaking to you then. Goodbye"

Let him disconnect from the call first.

Call back on the day and time you agreed.

Remember you are judged by what you say and do. Be reliable.

Perfecting The Art Of Telesales *Spiced With The Magic Of Neuro-Linguistic Programming*

Here is an example of a very basic introduction to help you get started.

Remember to listen to how he sounds when he answers the phone. 'Match' his voice and tone. If he says "**Hello** Bloggs here" Say "**Hello** Mr. Bloggs" rather than "Good morning Mr. Bloggs":

"Good morning/afternoon Mr.... this is ...of... ".

Now qualify that he is the right M.A.N (money/authority/need), and he is responsible for authorizing as well as purchasing your kinds of products/services". (You are trying to establish what involvement this person has in the buying process and if he has any needs. If he is not the one with the needs, find out who has them, and seek his help to gain access to him. Ask to be transferred. **People love to help**.)

"Can you assist me please, are you the person who authorizes the purchase of xx products/services for your company?" Wait for the answer.

Followed by -

"Are you familiar with our organization?"

Or

"I am sure you have heard of us"

If he answers "yes". Ask, "What has he heard?"
(You do not want to spend time later in the call telling him things that he already knows about your company, instead you can tell him new, exciting and relevant things he doesn't know, which may be of interest.)

Or ask -

"What impressions do you have of our company?"
(His perception of your company may be important, as his views may be incorrect. You may need to help him revise his perceptions particularly if they are negative.) Wait for answer - (if he has not heard of you, give a **very brief** description of your organization.) Avoid talking too long. Your prospect is the one who needs to be talking.

Commit to conversation.

"The purpose of my call is to introduce you to xxxx company and secondly how you and your company may benefit from utilizing our. ......products/services".

Please note!

A more sophisticated and interesting introduction will stimulate and engage your prospect's emotions quicker; however, this requires sound preparation. To make it relevant and interesting means you will need to do thorough pre-call planning.

1. Find something about his organization that will stimulate his interest, then you can say things like..

"I read about..." or "I saw..." or "I heard about your exciting... and this is where I believe we could assist you (save time and money/stay ahead of your competition)" "I noted from an article I read in... that you are interested in...we have experience in this area". Now immediately you have stated the relevant fact about his company, ask an 'open interest question' this will help you keep control and maintain the conversation flow and get him talking. Commit him to conversation, "So tell me about how ..."

Or,

2. Use third-party reference stories and multiple hooks as to why he should listen to you.

"This is ...(your name) with...(your company). Thank you for taking time to speak with me, as we have been working with...(state the customers who are in a similar business to your prospect) for the last ...years (establishes your credibility) and when we started working with them their initial issues were x...y...z and we thought you might have similar experiences" (you could pause at this point and wait for a response).

If he says "no", i.e. he doesn't have those particular experiences, you could say "That is good to hear Mr...so what kind of things are you finding a challenge at this time?"

If he says "yes", i.e. his concerns are as you suggested, you can continue on... "And because we have been able to provide them cost-effective and time-saving products/services I wondered how interested you would be in knowing how we helped them?"

The purpose of the (multiple) hooks is to heighten the prospect's receptivity to listen to you. As the level of his curiosity rises to solve a problem he has not yet admitted having, so does his willingness to participate in the conversation.

The real skill is for you to get him to uncover:

- What the real problem is (Prospects often describe symptoms, which you may have to work through with him to help identify the true problem. Who has this problem, what specific affect it is having, and where in the organization it resides)

- Why it is a problem? (i.e. the impact it is having on his business)

- How long has he had it?

- How long is he prepared to put up with it?

- What are the consequences of taking action?

- What are the consequences of inaction?

- When does he intend to take action?

- And who will be involved in deciding what, when and how much they will commit to solve it?

- The 'how to solve it'…is what he buys – using your product/service

So heightened curiosity and a sense of urgency must be maintained throughout the telephone sales call.

Telling stories is a great way of opening up his unconscious neural networks of his brain, and giving references of how other customers solved similar problems using your product/service is a great way to gain his 'buy in' without the need of him being first.

Introductions

The first few seconds of a call are absolutely vital

Enough interest must be generated to encourage the prospect to listen further, and to participate in a conversation with you

Your introduction must include who you are, and the reason why you may have something that is beneficial to him, **without telling the prospect too much too soon**

Always double check, before you start the selling process, that you are presenting your products/services to the right person

This 'right' person needs to be someone who can:

1. Make the decision to buy!

Or

2. Seriously influence the decision to purchase

All introductions consist of the same ingredients:

-   A statement or claim (which must be factual and true). May be something you have read about him or his organization. Or perhaps a referral you have from someone he knows

-   Followed by a statement of what it means to him

Example:

"Good morning Mr…I am…from… I don't know if you are aware but we are now offering a service whereby you can buy… from us direct, had you heard anything about this?

Wait for a response, which is likely 'no' otherwise you wouldn't be calling.

Then continue "Well obviously this can mean huge savings as you will be able to buy at wholesale prices. The reason for my call today is to introduce myself and see how our new service can benefit you…so I wonder can you help me on a few points please…" Now ask an **open relevant** question…

Consider the different introductions you may need. Prepare attention/interest generators.

A cold call: A company or person with whom you have never had contact, or the contact was a long time ago.
A warm call - A company or person on your list who has had some kind of contact from you or your company.
A referral call – A colleague or someone has recommended that you call the prospect.
Prospecting into an existing customer call

Example of introduction to an existing customer:

"Good afternoon Mr...this is ...from...you purchased a...from us a couple of weeks ago, that is right isn't it? (The purpose of this question is to get him involved and committed to the conversation, remind him he is already a customer, not to show that you didn't know he had purchased something from you.) His "yes" response will be quick, so be ready to continue with your statement...

"As part of our after sales service, we like to contact you and check everything went smoothly, and that you are happy with the service so far?" Wait for response, and then cover any points he raises. Then..."Since you appear to be happy with...I wonder what you had considered our...(if there is an add-on product)...?" If not..."who else in the organization could benefit from this; can you help on a few names please?". (Note: If you use this kind of introduction to a follow on sales call, **do check** service delivery before you make the call. If there have been any problems you need to know **before you call** the customer.)

Perfecting The Art Of Telesales *Spiced With The Magic Of Neuro-Linguistic Programming*

Creating interest

The objective of the 'have' and 'want' questions is to arouse interest and establish what he needs. **Want** - establishes **desired state**, *have* - establishes **current state** **The gap** is the wants/needs.

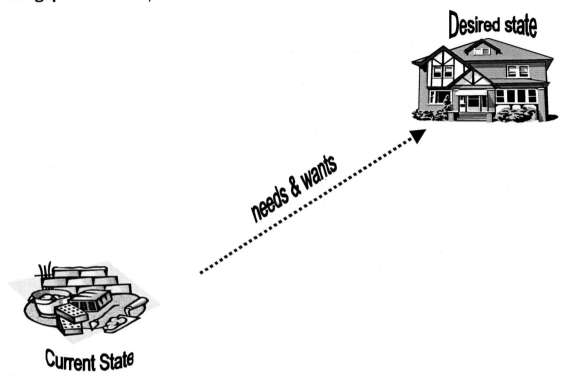

The objective of fact-finding is to establish a business need or a desired end result. In all teleselling it is imperative to gain attention and interest quickly. As previously advised:

-   Thorough fact-finding is important as it influences the rest of this and future sales. Fact-finding must be conversational and not an interrogation

-   By being and sounding enthusiastic and showing interest, you will prompt the prospect to talk easily about his needs

-   Something a prospect likes to do is talk about himself

-   It is your job to guide and control the conversation

-   Ask logical and open questions (Remember qualification)

-   Actively listen to the answers

-   Use the information that you are being given to build your case

-   Take notes

Remember:

- He is not always clear himself about what he wants. You are there to help him open his mind and come to decisions, so ask him relevant and interesting questions that prompt him to talk

- To ask about the costs of what he is doing or intends to do. Or indeed what 'inaction' will cost him or his company

This is how you build your case for him to spend money with you.

If you do not find out what costs he incurs through either not changing something or 'inaction' then you cannot justify him spending money on your products/services.

It is important to get a broad understanding of the company's current business status, the challenges that management face; for example expanding the business, making it more efficient, making it more profitable, increasing market share, and so on.

It is up to you to assess with him which of his challenges it is most appropriate to pursue.   If the need is not a priority there will be no compulsion to purchase your product/service. This is why you have to help create a sense of urgency. Find something that will compel him to move towards fulfilling his needs/wants. For example, new legislation, existing regulatory deadlines, his competition taking a new product to market.

Avoid stopping at the first sign of an opportunity - keep probing across all areas of the business he is concerned with.

A trap a lot of telesales people fall into is to find 'a problem' and then jump straight to a solution.

The effect of this is:

- Valuable qualification information is missed
- The extent of all his needs are not explored

The prospect sees you as a 'telesales person' rather than a business person who will be able to help him now and in future.

Examples: - general qualification questions (these apply to most companies and fact-finding situations):

The list is not exhaustive nor are the questions in logical order - you would not start the conversation focused on the money. These have been written in MANDACT as an easy way to remember how to cover all the bases within the teleselling process, and provide examples of how questions can be structured.

- You will need to write your own questions in a way that makes you feel confident in asking them

- They need to be written in a logical order within your presentation

- Please note sometimes your prospect is so busy giving you information he answers your questions without the need for you to ask them

- So pay attention, do not make him repeat himself

- Do remember to clarify what you are told, paraphrase your understanding and keep building agreement and commitment

Your personality is key, how I would ask and how you may ask will be entirely different.

Test different ways of asking and listen to the responses. Keep changing them until they feel right for you.

A reminder:

Whether this prospect has an interest or not... always look for other prospects for your product/services – someone else in his organization...or someone he knows in another organization.

Always ask, "Who else in your company (or that you know) could benefit from knowing about these products/services?" Be on the look out for more suspects.

M What budget do you have for purchasing xxx products/services?

What is the average spend each year for these types of products/services?

What kind of benefits did you gain from previous purchases of xxx products/services?

A What do you do as a company? (If it is not obvious or you have not bothered to research, use this information to promote other products/services that may relate to his specific business)

Who normally authorizes and organizes purchases of xxx products/services within your organization?

Who is involved in the decision-making process for these types of purchases, and what role do they each play?

What other responsibilities do they have?

N What plans do you have for increasing sales?

What plans do you have for moving the company towards...?

What plans do you have for moving the company away from...?

What plans have you to bring new technology in...?

What plans do you have for implementing... (whatever it is your products/services do)?

What xxx requirements have you to fulfil in the next six months?

*What is important about this? *Why is it important?
(*The answers to these two questions will give you the true value he places on the solution to his problem and real motivation to solve it)

What have you done about finding the solutions?

What kind of xxx products/services are you specifically interested in?

What kinds of products/services have you a feel for, already looked at, heard about or trialed? (Some companies send out trials of their products. An example of this is an Internet Service Provider. ISPs often send unsolicitored CD's of their service for people to try out i.e. trialling)

So you have realised that by solving this particular problem it will also benefit others, is that right? So what will this mean for you/your organisation?

Perfecting The Art Of Telesales *Spiced With The Magic Of Neuro-Linguistic Programming*

D How does the planning process work in practice for the organizing and purchasing of xxx product/service?

What is your purchasing policy on the use of xxx products/services?

When do you review suppliers?

What criteria to do use for assessing suppliers?

What do you do regarding a supplier's shortcomings?

What do you know about our products/services?

Once a decision has been made, what internal procedures will be followed prior to placing an order with the chosen supplier?

A What resources do you have available to implement/organize for this solution?

How much help do you anticipate you may need?

How much budget has been set aside for additional consultancy, training and implementation?

C Who else have you approached regarding a solution?
(It is likely that he will have approached an incumbent supplier)

When?

How far are you with them? (Meaning how far down the purchase cycle, if they are about to sign an order...maybe you are chasing a need that no longer exists. You have to decide if it is a good use of your time to try and change his mind at this very late stage...only you can decide)

Who in the organization is not supporting the changes that are necessary? How can I help you with this?

T What is your timescale for this solution?

What will happen if you do not meet your deadline? (If this is a short timescale you are looking for flexibility to be able to meet it, otherwise you may conclude this is a need that cannot be fulfilled by you)

List open 'relevant' questions for your presentation

A cold call:

A warm call:

A referral call:

An existing customer:

Perfecting The Art Of Telesales *Spiced With The Magic Of Neuro-Linguistic Programming*

Examples confirmation/clarification questions:

- "So your company does have a central purchase set up?"

- "Have I got this correct, you said each department can purchase autonomously?"

- "Do you want to ask me any specific questions about our products/services?"

- "If I were to provide relevant testimonials you will be happy to make this purchase?"

- "If I were to show you a way in which this will save you time and money you will be happy to go ahead?"

- "Does this sound sensible to you so far?"

When you gather information it is important to reconfirm his interest on his answers.

"What will it take for you to solve this situation? (Get his wish list) If I can show you a way to...to what extent would that be of interest to you?"

You encourage decisions.

"What if you were also able to...?"(Add value)

A final question must be closed to confirm real interest, i.e. you seek a 'yes'.

"So if you were able to (state need) then you will be able to (state benefit or desired end result). Is this what you are saying?"

He will agree if your assessment of the situation is correct.

If your assessment is correct and he agrees then next comes knowledge of your products/services being extended and suitability appreciated

Continue and inspire him...(remember to listen for and use sensory-based language. **(see pp. 145-181)** use such phrases as....

"Let me explain step by step..." "Let us imagine..." " Let me tell you about our ...products/services" "Let me give you a feel for how it works...." "What it all boils down to is this...."

Leading to...

Building his desire to buy your products/services means you have to match the value of your products/services to his specific needs, wants, desires, plans etc.

You are employed to sell his (the prospect's) business to his market (his customers), ensure his company's continuity, increased profits, and market share through the use of your products/services.

Remember his buying motives: - profit, prestige, continuity and because of his competition.

Unless motivated by the idea of how your products/services play a part in helping his business (or him personally) he will not be motivated to purchase your products/services.

Empathy is needed - bringing him into the technicalities of the decision-making, i.e. plan together.

Use appropriate language to ensure you are really making yourself understood.

Question him when you do not understand.

As you establish his needs, commit your prospect to them, and continue to probe until your fact-finding is complete.

When you are sure you have all the facts you are then in a position to introduce your products/services and to explain how these will meet his needs.

Perfecting The Art Of Telesales *Spiced With The Magic Of Neuro-Linguistic Programming*

Creating desire

This is the point at which you explain your products/services, their features and benefits and customer appeal.

Benefits: - advantages or profit - what it will do for him specifically. (Note: advantages are not need-specific but benefits are.)

Too often, telesales people describe the features of a product/service, and not what is in it for the prospect, or what the product/service will mean to him specifically.

Therefore, you need to ensure that you match his need with the relevant benefit and put that benefit across in such a way that it builds up his desire to buy – known as customer appeal.

An example: Prospect's statement of need:

"I want something that is 'easy to use' whilst I am 'on my travels'. I cannot afford a laptop computer, and I have limited keyboard skills anyway but I need to be able to 'record information'". (His specific needs (desired end result) are "ease of use", "on my travels", "record information")

You - gain his agreement that your understanding is correct:

"So you are really looking for a compact unit that is flexible and portable with easy input, it that right?" Wait for a yes.

Feature (What it is): "Mr.... we have a pen pad...

Advantage (What it has that might be of benefit): Battery operated, so fully portable, hand-held and pen-based input, and never runs out of paper. Easy to use.

Benefit (What it does specifically for him), and **customer appeal** (image or emotion it creates when he owns it). This is what he wants to hear about so you continue with...

Which means that: "It is so compact and 'easy to use'. It's portable so you will 'be able to record information' no matter where your 'travels' take you, and that is exactly what you are looking for isn't it?" Get agreement. Get him to say 'YES'. Sell him **benefits and use his words.**

Remember - business people buy end results a lot faster than the product/service itself. When you find out the desired end result sell your product/service to it.

E.g. Not everyone wants a mobile telephone but everyone does want a fast and easy means of keeping in touch with others.

Perfecting The Art Of Telesales *Spiced With The Magic Of Neuro-Linguistic Programming*

Remember, he is only interested in what your product/service does for him or his organization.

The easiest way to prove the worth of anything is to relate relevant benefits to the specific needs of your prospect.

Make sure there is a definite commitment from the prospect, gain agreement from him; otherwise you will have trouble later committing him to action.

Feature	(What it has)	Are facts about the product/service, which are provable and true
Advantage	(What it does)	Are benefits that are not specific to a prospect's need but he will get them anyway
Benefits	(What it will do for the prospect specifically)	In relation to need... leading to
Customer appeal		The images and emotion created once owned.

Write out the features advantages and benefits of your products/services

Feature (What it is)	Advantages (What it does)	Benefit (What it will do for him specifically)	Which means that	Customer appeal (Image or emotion created once owned)

Example: "So Mr... my understanding of your requirements are A...B...C...
is that correct? Wait for his answer. It needs to be 'yes'. If 'no', then seek
clarification, reconfirm and summarize understanding of the requirement again
before continuing ... you must have a **'yes'**. (You must have the real
requirements.)

"Great, well this is how (state company) and our products/services can help
you".

Now state how you can help him by explaining the features/benefits and **tag
them** back to his needs, then state, "which is what you want isn't it?" You
need to get another **'yes'**. (This is called building the **'yes set'**. Once he starts
to say **'yes'**, it becomes harder for him to say 'no'.)

After completing your recommendations you must tell him the cost of your
products/services with the relevant benefits.

Do not wait for him to ask.

During the course of the conversation your prospect will have said things that
indicate his interest; these are known as buying signals.

Buying signals are any sound indication or question asked, showing that the
prospect may be interested. They should be actively listened for and dealt with
appropriately, e.g. the prospect asks a question, and, often, it is good to get
some form of commitment by asking him a question too.

This means you can 'test close' your sale at this point.

Examples of what to listen for:

- What is the price?
- When do I pay?
- When can it be delivered/implemented?
- If he asks advice
- When he asks you questions
- Asks about companies that use your products/services
- Ratio of open/closed questions he asks
- Ask specifics
- Ask for references
- Thinks out loud where he can get the money
- Asks about future developments of products/services
- What discounts you give
- How is it purchased?
- Statements of intent will often be indications of **'psychological ownership'**,
  e.g. "when the service comes up for renewal" rather than **"if"**. These
  indications can be misleading so you must reassure the prospect and verify
  the signal, e.g. "You seemed to be interested in...is this correct?"

List buying signals that are relevant to your product or service

Test closing - examples:

He says "Do I get a 10% discount?"

Your response (if you give discounts) would be (test close) "Do you want to buy it if we do?"

This way you have not committed to the discount but you are asking the prospect to commit to purchase if you do.

He says "When do you deliver?"

You say "When do you need delivery?"

He says "Every two weeks".

You say, and **test close and then close**, "Great then we will deliver every two weeks, which day would you like the first delivery made?"

He says "Thursday next".

You say "Thursday it is".

You deal with all the relevant ordering details and **thank** him for the order.

Perfecting The Art Of Telesales *Spiced With The Magic Of Neuro-Linguistic Programming*

Action - the final stage in the sales process

Getting decisions in your favour – another 'YES' to something

You have made a coherent presentation and your prospect is still awake, this is a good sign. However, it is no good going through all the steps of the call unless you are prepared to ask for the order or next action. (I must add at this point, that this process of closing more often takes place over several calls, and made fairly closely together – or at least with the prospect's agreement to dates and times to call back.)

Your prospect expects you to close and ask for the order or next action. If you do not, and you sound hesitant, he will wonder why you bothered with all this discussion.

(It is imperative that you have him take an action, or set an expectation that he has to do something…getting him to actively participate will be the reason for your next call if you have to make one.)

As long as you believe that you have proved a true need, and have the relevant product/service to satisfy his requirement, then closing is the only thing left to do.

Fan the flames of desire (the higher and more intense the fire the more the customer will pay for a fire extinguisher, as it were.)

You are there to help your prospect, and turn him into a customer!

Close quickly – the customer gets the benefit if we close quickly. So how soon should he have the benefit?

It is the final step in the process - getting a decision to move forward and motivating him from desire to positive and immediate action. He expects to be asked to make a decision about something.

You will have spent a great deal of time trying to convince him about the merits of your product/service.

He also expects you to advise him of the next logical step. So tell him.

Remember the purpose of all this is to direct his thoughts and preoccupation to your product/service.

If you avoid asking for a decision, what was the point of your call!

If you omit to ask for a 'next action' it has all been a waste of time.

Your job is to make the prospect aware of his needs and desires. If you have proved a need and have a solution – ask for the business.

If you paid attention during your conversation there will have been various signals given out by the prospect, in a form of questions, buying signals, and even objections that will have allowed you to assess his thinking.

However, the product/service you have recommended possibly represents a considerable sum of money out of his budget. It may be necessary to break down the price so that he can relate to the costs of his current method of purchasing a similar product/service. For example, if you are selling training programmes, ask him to consider the investment as a per head rate rather than a total price. If selling computer software, then a per user rate rather than the value of the total license (i.e. £5000 becomes £500 per head for 10 course participants or software users respectively.)

If he has doubts you must put his fears into perspective and show how the benefits outweigh the costs involved.

There may be a combination of motives and quite often he will not give a reason for interest.

Your job is to establish what he needs; reinforce his desires and convince him that your product/service is the best solution.

Example:

"Isn't it true that as we are planning this training programme today it saves you time and leaves you free to concentrate on more important matters. It controls your costs because you know what you are paying for in advance. So when is the best time for you do this course, February or April?"

The purpose of asking a tie-down question "isn't it true...wouldn't you agree" is to test the true response of your prospect to your suggestion.

The 'close' commits him into making the decision of which month is or is not best for him to do this training.

Having asked an alternative-closing question like this "when would you like to do this February or April" keep quiet until he answers and makes his decision.

The alternative close gives him a choice of **when he does it, not if he does it!**

When he accepts - you have a new customer.

If you have misunderstood the conversation, or misread the signals he has been giving, or missed his earlier objections and still attempted to gain a decision, then he will resist and raise another objection.

Skilful questioning during the call will often allow you to overcome objections before they are raised. However, if they do come up at a later stage, they must be handled immediately.

Objections do not always mean 'no'.

They are brought up for various reasons. The prospect

- Needs time to think

- Is trying to outsmart you

- Genuinely has a problem

- Is stalling for time

- May even be wanting to go ahead but needs something clarified

An objection is a buying signal - it is another opportunity to sell.
Recognize objections for what they are: a stalling tactic (an excuse or a real problem), a true concern, or just to put his mind at rest before he says 'yes'.

Avoid being too clever with your answers; you are there to help him. But do qualify what he really means by what he said, rather than just accepting what he says at face value!

Prospects rarely say what they really mean, and on the phone remember 'the meaning' of the communication is only given in the words and tone. The non-verbal cues that you depend upon are missing (body language, which makes up 55% of how meaning is communicated). You have to get into the habit of asking for clarification to get precise and factual information.

There is more on meaningful communication **(see pp. 132-144.)**

Why your prospect may say 'yes'. He

- Likes you (It is imperative that he does)
- Wants to own what you have to offer
- Thinks it will benefit his company
- Fears that, if he doesn't buy now, he will have to pay more later on
- Cannot resist the word 'new'
- Likes spending money
- Is not happy with his present supplier and wants a change
- Is in a hurry
- Thinks it will make him look good
- Likes making bold decisions
- Has heard that a rival has done well with your services and wants to get in on the act
- Does not have the courage to say 'no'
- Feels insecure
- Is impressed by what you have done for others
- Needs, or thinks he needs your products/services
- Is happy and in the right mood
- Is afraid someone else will beat him to it

He has an

- Automatic convincer channel - makes decisions easily and quickly
  (In a work context approx. 8% of the population decide in this way.)

Why your prospect may say 'no'. He

- Does not like you (little chance of a sale)
- Has not been listening
- Only wanted to find out if you had any good ideas
- Is prejudice against your company
- Fears making decisions
- Does not have the authority to make decisions
- Does not have any money
- Is afraid of the consequences of saying 'yes'
- Is tired and in an unresourceful mood
- Does not like change
- Has not understood your presentation
- Hopes you will come back and improve your offer
- Does not like the features of your products/services
- Is worried about your after sales service
- Does not like your company or your boss

He has a

- Number of Times convincer
  (In a work context approx.52% of people decide in this way)

- Consistent convincer channel
  (In a work context approx. 15% people decide in this way)

- Period of Time convincer channel
  (In a work context approx. 25% of people decide in this way)

(Convincers see pp. 167-8)

Remember it is important to keep building the **'yes sets'**

He may never admit any of the above

The reasons he may say 'no' will be disguised by the objections he raises

You have to question him further until you can get him to make his objection specific – then you can deal with it

Poor telephone selling creates objections – the real solution to this is not to become better at handling objections but to improve the presentation so they do not occur.

Many telesales people believe that if they had better answers to objections their results would improve.   This may be true for some, but it does not matter how brilliantly the objection is handled, it has still created a gap between the telesales person and their prospect.   Rapport will probably need building again.

Emphasis should be placed on more skilful questioning and qualification.

For example: -

The prospect says "I need to take this to my director".   This means he is not the sole decision maker (if a decision maker at all).   Thorough qualification would have highlighted this and the telesales person would not be trying to gain a decision from someone who has no authority to make it!

So, objections are usually the point at which most telesales people learn the real art of selling.

The majority of objections are not inherent to the prospect, but are created by the behaviour of the telesales person.   A common situation is where the telesales person assumes he has found a need, and seeing the opportunity proceeds to sell the product/service on that need and creates an objection.

Whereas, a telesales person who holds back on offering a solution until he has built strong desire, not only receives fewer objections – he closes more sales.

In preparation for dealing with objections it is wise to list every reasonable objection that you ever encounter, and as you continue your teleselling add any new ones that throw you off balance.   Set up these objections as targets to overcome: a positive selling point will always overcome a weak objection.   If you are well prepared and become skilful at questioning it means you will encounter very few objections.

There are in general three classes of objections:

1. **Real** – this must be handled. If unsatisfied, your prospect keeps it in mind and it prevents him from paying close attention to anything else you are saying.

2. **Imaginary** – He may raise an objection that has no real substance. These types of objections come up for a variety of reasons – a mild way of expressing irritation at being disturbed, to show he is not easily won over, to display a sense of humour or quick wit. It has so little foundation it can often be treated by pleasantly agreeing completely with the prospect and then offsetting the objection with a counter remark in the same category. Here are two examples I personally experienced:

Prospect in a Stockbroker

"You are the 348th telesales person that has called me this quarter".

My response: "Really, Mr...that is an interesting statistic what would you like me to do with this information?" (Said with a smile in my voice.) He laughed with surprise. It was clear he was not expecting a fast and coherent response, thinking his comment would throw me and it didn't. We had a great conversation and he agreed to hear about the service on offer, and eventually he bought from me. This took several calls, over several weeks - but he bought. I doubt my service was any better than others who may have called him; the difference was I stood out from the crowd, which gave me an opportunity to present my services. This is all I could possibly expect.

Prospect in Life Assurance Company

She said with obvious distaste (I could hear it in her tone - like she had a bad smell up her nose) "I get people like you calling me all the time, I'm not interested."

My response: "I know just how you feel, I say the same thing every time one of your sales people call me".   I said this with a smile on my face. She laughed out loud and said "Point taken". We chatted. She didn't buy, but she gave me a hearing.

3. **Excuses:** They are an attempt to postpone action. Often they are not worth any thought just keep on selling.

**Common sales
resistances**

1.   Authority to purchase

You sell too much which means he is put off. You must re-examine closely
his needs.

2.   Change

There is a natural resistance against unfamiliarity. Anything different arouses
suspicion. When examining resistance there are 5 considerations:

1.	Risk	Handling fear of the unknown - testimonials
2.	Effort	Make it easy for him to buy - detail quote and gain his participation
3.	Satisfaction	Give convincing reasons for product/service
4.	Initial Cost	Postpone cost questions until the end of the sale – cost is meaningless until needs are fully analysed
5.	Criticism	Overcome his fear of being criticised for changing his policy Credit for wise decision- making

When faced with resistance never use any form of pressure on your prospect.
Instead, involve him by asking his views and advice. Use participation and make
your proposition prospect-centred.

3.   Time

Do not proceed if his tone or manner or further questioning antagonizes him.
Use your judgement.

If he believes it is the wrong time but the right product/service then you need to
establish when he believes the time will be right and need to show, by
testimonials, that the present time is always a good decision.

4.   Expenditure

Compared with what is your product/service too expensive?
If he sees it as too expensive, it has to be in comparison with something else,
or what he thinks he is prepared to spend on it.

You need to get him to view price objectively - offer value for money. Strongly
sandwich price between benefits.

Show how investment in your product/service gives a return.

Rules for handling objections:

- They must be anticipated and prepared for

- Listen (never interrupt, let him have his say) and then isolate the objection i.e. confirm it is his only objection/concern!

- Ask back - clarify excuse or real objection – get him to make his objection specific. Better still jolt him into answering his own objection. Get him to transform his objection into a suggestion

- Commit to purchase - answer the true objection. You could just ignore an excuse

- Remember to ask for the action again - ask for the order

Remember: You are building a staircase of agreement. You have to re- build on things to which he agreed, so show how you and he are both striving for the same end.

Accelerate his desire, make him see the benefits are so pronounced he forgets the pain of parting with his money. Inflate the value and deflate the price. Prove he is buying a product/service of value.

Always keep cool. Your calmness will impress your prospect and make you master of the situation.

Tips for handling real objections:

- Acknowledge his point of view

- Move to qualify that you understand it correctly – so paraphrase what you have understood and let him confirm

- Serious objections will revolve around his true needs

- Overcome objections by satisfying his concerns and by matching his key decision criteria

- Take care to deal with the entire list of requirements

By answering his real objections and matching relevant benefits of your product/service with his needs, you will win agreement.

Be thankful for objections (buying signals). They make you think. Sharpen your wits and your technique. Even if you lose this sale you have gained knowledge, understanding and wisdom – you are better prepared for the next call.

A technique for establishing if this is a true or false objection

Objections fall into distinct categories based on the prospect's buying decisions, which are need, product, the source of supply, you (and your proof), price and time.

You need to determine which type of objection it is, or perhaps a combination of them.

If, for example, you **assume** you have a price objection when the real hidden concern is time or source of supply objection, you will be giving the wrong response!   Then he will raise another objection.

You must always make your prospect clarify what he means by what he says. Get him to be specific about his concern. **Never assume anything – ASK!**

Objections are either excuses to get out of this conversation and off the phone, or has he a real reason for not purchasing?

- Listen to the objection

- Qualify that it is the only concern (i.e. isolate the objection - establish if that is all that stands between you and his decision to purchase)

- Seek clarification - ask it back - question it. Several things can happen:

1. As he attempts to clarify his objection, he realizes that his concern is unfounded, or it even sounds stupid to him so he gives up trying to justify it to you

2. He may talk himself out of the objection if you let him!

3. He may change his objection to something entirely different (which means if you had responded to his initial objection, your answer would not have appeased him: he would have just raised another objection)

Do remember, however, he may or may not have a workable solution, and if you involve him in the process of finding it, he will be working with not against you. If the same objection comes back, and he has clarified what he meant by what he said, then answer it.

Only answer **real** objections:

- Commit to next stage (if it is an excuse it will change or go away, he could be just airing his views and will be content when he has done so)

- Explain the capability of your product or service and the value in purchasing, and make it relevant to his needs, wants and desires

- Ask another closing question (ask for the order) and stay quiet!

- Your prospect will now be considering your proposition. Do not be panicked by a few seconds silence into speaking a flood of useless words

- Be patient. Keep quiet. The pressure is now on him to make a decision. Give him time to think

- Wait for answer

- Confirm and request the action for the order

- Check back details - the telephone number, names, and any other information that is relevant

- Always state your terms of business

- Summarize action

As you require action from the prospect, make sure your communication is clear about what you expect him to do to organize the purchase, and ask when he is going to be able to send any confirmation you require. Be that a purchase order, email, sending a cheque, or taking a credit card payment.

Tell the prospect what you intend to do, and when.

Check if he knows anyone else who may benefit from your products/services - get names and telephone numbers - seek other opportunities for business.

Remember to thank him for his time and for buying from you.

Example answers to common objections (which are usually excuses!)

Prospect: "I'm too busy to talk to you"

You: "Mr...it's impossible for me to do justice to my proposition in just a few words. It is a very important product/service and may turn out to mean a lot to you given time to explain..." now continue as if he never brought up the 'too busy' objection.

Now a couple of things:

1. If you continue on as if he has not said he was too busy, one of two things will happen, you will interest him and he will forget how busy he is. He will stop you and repeat his statement, or suggest you call him another time, either way, get agreement as to when you can call back, get a date and time. Call then.

2. When you first made the call, if he sounded distracted it would be better to check if it is convenient to continue (he then decides whether he is prepared to listen), and if not, gain agreement to call back and get a specific date and time to make the call. (Only you can judge which is the best approach to take. It is crucial that you listen to the atmosphere of what you hear as he answers the phone, and how he sounds.)

   Prospect: "Not interested" (often said as you first introduce yourself)

   You: "Mr...I can appreciate you receive many calls like this but I would not expect you to be interested in something that you have not had opportunity to investigate. However, I would appreciate the chance to put that right, if I get right to the point you can decide..." Now get to the point, make a beneficial statement/claim and ask a relevant open question...commit him to the conversation.

   Or if you cannot continue and would feel more comfortable calling back..."We could fix a time for me to call you back; how about...or...?"

   Prospect: Not interested (during/after you have made your presentation)

   You: "I am sorry to hear this Mr...there must have been something I have missed here. Can I ask you what specifically **did not interest** you?" Wait for his answer... "Thank you for explaining and I can see why that is now, so what sorts of things are you looking for at present/or are important to you at this time?" (Do not draw breathe between any of these statements otherwise he will interrupt you. Increase the speed of speech so you state your whole question.) This question will get you back into fact-finding and you may establish there is something else you can help him with. Conversely, it may be he does not have any needs you can fulfil at this time.

When you cannot find a need, close the call politely, leaving the door open to go back some other time.

Never invite 'not interested' or 'no need' objections. When you fact-find well and listen actively, you are assessing if there are opportunities for your product or service and sometimes the prospect has no need for what you are offering.

So, say "Mr…I can see that my current offering does not suit you, but thanks for your time. May I keep in touch with you from time to time?" He will invariably say 'yes'.

This approach will demonstrate that you understood what you were being told. He will value your integrity and business acumen. Next time you call he will be just as pleased to talk with you and there may be an opportunity to pursue.

Too expensive

"Too expensive" could mean any of the following to your prospect:

- More expensive than he thought

- He wants a discount

- More money than he can authorize

- He has no budget

- He is not convinced he is getting value for money

- As a buyer it his job to get lower prices

- He is not the decision maker (Why are you speaking to this particular individual? You may have a valid reason, but if you know he is not the decision maker, do not ask him to make decisions he cannot make. Ask for commitment to things he can agree too)

- He does not want the product/service

- He knows of other suppliers who are cheaper

Therefore, you have to find out exactly what he means by "too expensive" in order to overcome the objection.

The need for clarification applies to every objection that is ever raised. Your prospect rarely says what he means, or what he is really thinking.

How to seek clarification:

Prospect: "It's too expensive"

You: "Mr...is this your only concern?" You must get a 'yes' to this
            question, if he says 'no'; he has other objections so have him tell
            you what they are.

Now ask back the objection:

You: "It's too expensive?" If you repeat back precisely the words he used and
            change your tone (use a rising inflection at the end of 'expensive') you will convert
            this statement into a question.

            Or,

            "May I ask in relation to what?"

            Or,

            "May I ask what exactly do you mean by that?"

            Or,

            "I am sure you have a good reason for saying that, please can you
            tell me what it is?"

            Make sure when you ask a question that you always soften your
            response with what we call **'soft front ends'**...

            "May I ask...?"?

            "I can appreciate why you think that..."

            "That is a very good point, I am glad you raised that..."

            "I see, this is the initial reaction of many of our customers..."

            "Perhaps I did not explain that point fully..."

            "If I can justify your spending that amount, would you be happy to go
            ahead?" (Of course, only say this if you can justify it.)

If his objection is true, and when he gives you his real (true) reason, give him
valid reasons in return (relevant benefits) for buying from you: tell him how the
advantages of your product/service outweigh the disadvantages!

Some prospects deliberately test you regarding price. Price and time objections
are the most common objections raised; they can easily throw you off balance,
so be prepared for them.

Perfecting The Art Of Telesales *Spiced With The Magic Of Neuro-Linguistic Programming*

The prospect's objective is to lower your expectations, to lower your aspiration level. Many are trained to do this, so never be put off.

Three principles in negotiating:

1. Never show anxiety or nervousness when you are asked about the price of your product/service

2. Your first response to the price challenge is to defend your price (which is not necessarily the right response, so make sure it is a price objection you are having to deal with)

3. If a concession is necessary - trade it

Negotiating means - what you offer him balanced by what he offers you.

Have alternatives available - your prospect must realize that if he wants to change the price, you will want to change the product/service.

To emphasize a point: -

Should it turn out **not** to be a price objection, then by asking back and seeking clarification it allows you to:

1. Answer his true concern, because he will have to clarify what he means and give you his real objection

2. Go back to fact-finding stage, establish a true need to which you can match your product/service, progress through the sale again, and close

Prospect: "I am happy with our present supplier"

You: Review supplier history:

"Fine Mr.... I can understand that, may I ask who they are?"

Prospect: "Fred Bloggs & Sons"

You: "And how long have you been using them?"

Prospect: 2 years

You: "So who were you using before that?"

Prospect: "Joe Soap and Daughters"

You: "And what were your reasons for switching?"
(He may say he doesn't know because did not choose the present supplier - so this means he is unable to make a real comparison. This means it is an excuse and not a real objection.) The prospect will be unable to continue on this tack and may be convinced your product/service is worth consideration, or he will give you his real objection.
If he did make the decision about the present supplier then continue...

Prospect: "Improved service, better prices...."

You: "And they lived up to your expectations?"

Prospect: "Yes"

You: "Well, if two years ago you were looking to improve results/prices, you considered the alternatives and made a switch, which worked well. Would you accept the possibility that the same thing could happen again?"

Prospect: "Yes"

You: "Well, it will take just a few minutes to explore that possibility."
Now continue with your proposition by asking him some more questions. Get him thinking and working towards the sale.

Or an alternative:

Prospect: "I am happy with our present supplier"

You: "Mr...just supposing you were convinced there was another
            supplier who could do more effectively and less expensively all the
            things you require, what would you do?"

            "Just supposing your present supplier for some reason, could not
            maintain supplies, what would happen?"

            "How long would it take you to get another supplier organized?
            Could you do it in time?"

            "Surely it would be more satisfactory to have two suppliers, then if
            anything happened to one of them, you could easily increase the
            business with the other.
            Besides, having two suppliers keeps them both on their toes."

Prospect: "I want to think about it"

You: "Mr...this is a very important decision you are about to make, and I
            am pleased you want to think it over; however, to clarify my thinking
            what is it you want to think about?"

-   Get him to list his concerns

-   Never leave the conversation not knowing what your prospect is 'thinking
    about'

-   If he has concerns/doubts or a real objection you need to know what it is

-   Now is the time to find out

    It needs to be said that if your prospect has a Period of Time convincer
    (**see p. 168**) then you will have to judge if he does need time to think about
    it. If you are sure he does and it is a true time objection ask "how much time
    do you need?" then agree a date and time to call back for his decision.

A recommendation:

I would certainly go through the "I want to think about it" objection handling technique at least once to help you decide if he is telling you the truth. Actively listen to his tone, i.e. what he says and the way he says it. Trust your instincts about what he says or doesn't say!

In fact, I think it is relevant to say at this point, that it is wise to attempt to overcome any objection at least twice before giving up. However, pay attention to the reaction of your prospect. Never antagonize him by being too persistent – use common sense and be sensitive.

Create your own clarification questions and answers to real objections
(Remember the soft front ends)

Objection	Question – ask it back to find out if it is an excuse or true objection	What would your answer be if it were a true objection?
Too Expensive		
No time		
I have seen a product like yours before I don't think it is value for money		

It's too complicated for what we need		
We have that service already		
We do...ourselves		

Add to your list new objections you need to find questions and answers for

Objection	Question – ask it back to find out if it is an excuse or true	What would your answer be if it were a true objection?

Closing over the telephone

- Your attitude is important. Be relaxed; your prospect needs to match your relaxed state of mind

- Remember you are calling to provide a product/service, so instruct him on how he can buy it. (He has buying procedures, you will have selling procedures. He will need to know what these are and the terms of business.)

- Repeat relevant benefits, the mind is influenced by repetition

- Check he understands what you are offering, demonstrate your interest in him and win his confidence. Keep your attitude in check, let him have his opinions and don't let them effect you. Be at cause and be natural

- Make sure he knows what else is on offer too. There may be other products or services he may find appealing, so watch out for opportunities to promote them

- Close the sale by suggestion. Through all your calls and presentations positive suggestion should be used. Make firm statements about your product or service so he always thinks positively about it. Ask questions that require the prospect to say 'yes'. Make it easy for him to accept a 'yes' decision

- Be quiet - keep your ears open, and concentrate. Silence has a great influence on him. It gives him chance to think, and if you have properly presented your product/service he will sell it to himself.

- Remember he is never sold; he buys what he thinks, and believes a product/service will do for him

The psychological moment to close the sale is any moment while you are in the act of telephone selling.

Closing techniques

Remember to keep control of every call - have a purpose for every call (i.e. to sell your products/services.)

Even when you talk to customers you know well - have a reason for the call and remember to close!

Be direct

"Shall I go ahead and order these for you now?"

"Shall we book in .... (specify a date) to commence the service?"

- This is the simplest close

- It will bring to light any hidden or unspoken objection

Assume (This is the only time I advocate the use of assumption, in test closing and closing. In general it is always better to ask than ever assume, but in selling it can be extremely useful.)

"May I go ahead and put the delivery down for Thursday?"

"Should I add Mr. x to our list of attendees too?"

Use alternatives

- This is a close when Mr.. is sitting on the fence and a push in the right direction will close the sale

- This close must start with the words "which do you prefer". Offer him a choice of doing this or that but not a choice of whether he does it or not

"Which would you prefer, delivery on Friday or Monday?"

Ask a direct question

- This can be used when Mr...says anything that means he does not want to buy now

Prospect: "I want to think about it"

You: "Mr... am glad you want to think about it, we are talking about a very important aspect of your company's business and I realize the need for caution, but to put my mind at rest may I ask you exactly what you are going to think about?"

- Wait for his answer

- Or another way is for you to list possible reasons. When you do, wait for the answer to each of your suggestions, and when you find the objection, answer it and close.

  Note: The first option is the better method, your prospect has to do all the thinking and talking. The pressure is on him.
  The second method I would avoid because, if you list the possible reasons not only does it mean you are under pressure to consider what those reasons may be, you may never identify the true reason. It is also a lengthy method of finding what his concern is. It is better to ask him, and put the pressure on him to give you his true reason.

Overcome caution

- This can be used when Mr....is ready to buy, but is afraid to say so

Prospect: "Can I have a 5% discount?"

You: Instead of simply saying yes, say,
             "If I give you this discount will you order today?"

- Wait for his answer, which has to be yes

Summarize to a close

- This is a close to use when you have answered all his objections, but he will still not make up his mind

- Instead of asking - tell him

You: "We have agreed that you want xxx product/service.
We have agreed that it will be the right time and that it will help increase productivity. The only decision you have to make today Mr... Is do you want, or do you not want, to save time and increase productivity?" (You state relevant benefits.)

Prospect: "Yes"

You: "Then let us order it now!"

Closing on a final objection

- By using this technique you have the chance of turning his objection to your advantage, and close the sale

- Hear him out. Do not interrupt

- Re-state the objection

You: "I see Mr..., so what you are saying is that you don't feel xxxxx will increase productivity. That is what you are saying isn't it?"
Confirm his objection. So if it wasn't for that you would go ahead, wouldn't you?"

Prospect: "Yes"

You: Question the objection

"Just to help me, why do you think that?"

- Wait for answer, answer any points raised, justify your product/service with benefits and ask for the order again, and keep your mouth shut. Wait for him to say, "Yes ok we'll go ahead"

Minor point to a close

- "I'll put your name on our provisional list and send the order form - may I just check your address?"

Create your own closing statements

Direct	
Assumptive	
Alternative	
Direct question	
Overcome caution	
Summary to a close	
Closing on final objection	
Minor Point	

Summarize action

When you get your prospect's commitment always:

-   Repeat back the details

-   Check names, addresses, telephone numbers, delivery times etc

-   Tell your prospect (or now new customer) what you intend to do, and by when

-   If you require action from the prospect, make sure your communication is clear, and ask when he is going to be able to provide you with whatever it is you require e.g. purchase order number

-   Always ensure the prospect understands your company's terms of business

-   **Never miss the opportunity to ask the prospect if he knows of anyone else that may be interested in your product/service and get the details**

-   Finally thank the prospect for the order/business and close the call with a firm goodbye

Always allow the prospect to disconnect the call first. Why? In case he thinks of something else to ask/tell you. A telephone call being disconnected by you first may sound abrupt, and give the impression that you are disinterested and in a hurry to get on with your next sales opportunity.

Follow up after the call

-   It is important that you do what you say you will

-   If you have agreed to call him with information and you cannot meet the agreed deadline, call him and advise of progress (even when there has not been 'any progress')

-   It costs the price of a phone call to keep him happy!

The only thing he will take away from your telephone sales call apart from information about a new product/service, or having agreed to purchase it, is the experience of how you provided the service. Make the experience positive and memorable. Stand out from the telesales crowd – be unique.

The follow-up telesales call

The second call increases your chances of success. Remember follow-up calls are every bit as important as the first call, and you need to handle them professionally and in a controlled way.

The structure of the follow up call has little difference to that of the first call – use AIDA. The same rules apply. The only other considerations are:

1. You will have arranged and agreed the call back (time and date) with your prospect. Make sure you call when you promised. Be prompt and show that you are reliable.

   The best time for a call back is about 3 days (so the prospect does not cool off); however, you have to respect the wishes of your prospect too, so sometimes you will have to accept his decision on date of the call back

2. If you have sent information

   - Refer back to last call; remember he does not have your notes or instant recall of the conversation
   - Refresh his memory
   - Repeat back what he told you
   - If you have sent out information, never, that is **NEVER** ask – "Have you read it?" or "Did you receive it?" These are closed questions, giving him he opportunity to say "no" and end the call.
   - Draw him in – build rapport - use open questions or a reference to something he may have looked at, listened to, or had opportunity to work through or agreed to do, or make a decision

     Example: ('Match' how he answers the phone, tone and words) if he says "Hello" you say "Hello" if he says "Good afternoon" you say "Good afternoon"... "Mr...you will remember I called you on Tuesday about xyz and I sent the information that you requested I am sure you noticed on page...the specific...that you were to discuss with..."

     Now ask more questions if you need to or continue to talk about benefits 'which means that'...and link into to asking again for a next action or order.

3. Remember ABC –**A**lways **B**e **C**losing

   - Remember to ask for the order – do it positively
   - Finish every call on a positive note regardless of outcome
     Gain a commitment to an agreed next step. Sales over the telephone are more often achieved via a series of incremental and important steps in each and every call.

Handling the incoming telesales call

It was once said that in one day Sampson slew 1000 Philistines with the jawbone of an ass. Every day millions of sales are killed with the same weapon!

More business is lost in the UK by poor handling of incoming telephone calls than for probably any other reason.

- Handle the incoming call professionally
- Answer within four rings
- **SMILE**, this helps your voice to sound more assertive and friendly
- Say good morning/afternoon
- Introduce yourself
- Obtain the caller's name then use it
  (If an incoming call is not convenient, explain why, take their name and number and offer to call back. Although I cannot think in what circumstances you would find it inconvenient to take an incoming sales call, it would be wiser not to answer the call if you are not prepared, than to ever tell a prospect or customer it is not convenient.)

Remember the structure of the telesales call – AIDA. This pattern works as well on the inbound as the outbound call. Incoming calls provide the **greatest opportunity for selling more** products/services!

Attention
- He called you - make sure you give your full attention
- He has to give you the reason for the call
- Qualify as much information as you can from him

Interest
- He has a high level of interest – he took the trouble to call you
- Seek opportunities. Do not just take orders
- Control the call
- Ask open questions
  (how, what, why, when, where and who)
- Actively listen (give verbal nods, make him feel connected to the conversation) and, resist the temptation to interrupt, give the conversation your undivided attention
- Make notes and repeat back information to the customer
- When you do speak 'voice/tone/word match'

Perfecting The Art Of Telesales Spiced With The Magic Of Neuro-Linguistic Programming

Desire - If it is the decision maker calling always focus on gaining the order, and/or *upselling/cross selling on products/services when you establish he has a real requirement.

- (If it is not the decision maker calling, find out who is calling, what their role is etc. and who has asked him to call – the decision maker or real influencer.) I would recommend that you make a call back to the person who has initiated the request, but only you can judge if this will be the appropriate thing to do. Whatever the situation, glean as much information as you can.

- There is no easier call on which to fact-find than the incoming call. The interest and desire level is high if he has taken time to call you.

Action - ASK for action NOW – an order or at least an agreement to call back to progress the sale.

- If you have to call back - remember to set him a task to perform – keep him active within this selling process. The more time and effort he expends, the more likely he is to buy.

- It is his actions, not your actions, which progresses the sale, unless you test his willingness to act, you will not know if he is serious.

*Upselling/cross selling means you make incremental sales based on other products/services you can provide to this particular customer, i.e. add-ons to the initial product/service purchase. You have to seek or point out these possibilities - the customer does not always see the relevance himself.

Remember - seek out other prospects for your products!

Minor points that can make or break a telesales call

- Be punctual - when telephoning prospects and customers. If you say "I'll call you at 11 am on Friday" - call on the dot - it suggests you are reliable and demonstrates professionalism

- When sending letters never let them go with a p.p. Instead, explain why you have not signed the letter yourself e.g. I'm leaving on business so my colleague will be signing this on my behalf.

- If sending an email – use the same business etiquette i.e. as if it were a letter

- Use the prospect/customer's name; remember a verbal handshake is as important as the handshake if you were meeting him

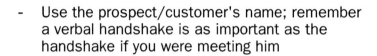

- Remember he has a preferred mode of communication. He processes via his senses. The prospect buys by his eyes, how he feels about your product/service, whether what you said made sense and how it sounded. When you send information, direct him to look at it,when you feel it is appropriate. Have him feel the texture of something, or walk through steps and procedures, make it sound enticing, that he cannot be without what you are offering. **(see pp. 145-161)**

- You attach value to your product/service by the way you talk about it/present it, or trial it

- Look after new customers. The end of the sale to you is just the start of a new product/service to this customer

- When you the have opportunity to meet a customer, be as professional face to face as you are on the telephone

- Always look the part - clean, tidy and co-ordinated

- Keep your desk tidy - clear away at the end of each day

- Prepare for tomorrow so you can start calling early in the day

- Sell yourself first

- Be happy to speak with people

- Smile – it's contagious!

- Use the terminology and language he uses

- Avoid expressing controversial viewpoints

- The best way to be interesting is to be interested

- Give him a reputation to live up to, and - more importantly - you live up to it

- Let him hear how others have helped you, not only how you have helped others

- Match him – voice, tone and movement, (although you will not see this happening)

- You cannot argue with ignorance – call another day – he will be in a different mood. **Prospects have behaviour, that is not who they are!**

- Always let him disconnect from the call first

Being an exceptional telesales person

You are a business person first!

- Creator
- Decider
- Communicator
- Organiser
- Negotiator
- Revenue and profit generator
- Business developer

Value yourself when talking to your prospect as the most valuable thing to happen to his business that day

He needs you, just as you need him

- He needs advice, your product/service and to solve a problem or respond to an opportunity
- Be assertive, act as an equal and show that you can work as a partner
- Work together to solve the problem and meet his needs

Organise your calls

- Prepare
- Be clear about the objectives that you need to satisfy
- If possible, avoid doing everything yourself. If you are a sole trader this is not easy, so you need to be highly organised, and thorough

Be trustworthy and truthful

- Establish long-term relationships through long-term actions
- Find out what your prospect/customer needs instead of trying to sell him what you have to offer
- Let your customer know that you can solve his problems – fairly and honestly
- TRUTH is one of the best weapons at your disposal
- Losing an 'inappropriate' sale in the short term may win you more in the long term because you win trust, respect and a loyal customer

Perfecting The Art Of Telesales *Spiced With The Magic Of Neuro-Linguistic Programming*

 Telephone selling is service

Time is money – be conscious of how you spend yours and your prospect's and customer's

 Telephone selling is really about people buying from you. All prospects and customers are doing is buying your desire to help. Make it easy for him to buy from you, and you will make your sales

 Be an active and effective listener – what will you learn? He will enjoy talking with you again

Think and act positively – be creative Make the experience he has with you, interesting, stimulating, exciting, and fun!

Be enthusiastic - leave him with a great feeling

You are unique so make yourself memorable!

Perfecting The Art Of Telesales *Spiced With The Magic Of Neuro-Linguistic Programming*

Building blocks for successful telephone selling

Enjoy telephone selling

It is simple - as long as you structure the conversation framework

People buy from people they like – build rapport

Features - **which means** - benefits   Paint word pictures

Be successful early in the day

Smile down the phone

Be an active listener

Use the prospect/customer's name

Control the conversation

Perfecting The Art Of Telesales *Spiced With The Magic Of Neuro-Linguistic Programming*

Educate yourself to be a professional (exceptional) telesales person

Do be professional at all times (your prospect/customer wants to talk about himself, his business, and his needs)

Utilise every telephone call to promote your products/services. Ask every prospect/customer to make decision to purchase (or at least a next step)

Convert every call into a sale and a means to progress the opportunity

Always ask for the order or a positive decision in your favour

Tenacity pays

Express yourself clearly and impress your prospect/customer in every situation

And remember...

Opportunities for sales are in **every** call you take or make - actively listen for them

Prospects and customers will love buying from you, and both of you will be winners

Part five

Adding Spice

Perfecting The Art Of Telesales *Spiced With The Magic Of Neuro- Linguistic Programming*

Adding spice to your telesales calls

Adding spice means providing you with a greater understanding of:

- Aspects of NLP as they relate to telephone selling

And a more conscious understanding of the aspects of:

- Meaningful communication

- Rapport building

- The use of sensory-based language

Aspects of NLP

NLP is the study of human excellence, a powerful and proactive approach to personal change.

Through a comprehensive study of NLP you will discover how to:

- Change
- Get motivated
- Achieve your goals
- Be more persuasive
- Eliminate fear and phobias
- Build self-confidence
- Increase self-appreciation and self-esteem
- Achieve peak performance

The possibilities are endless...and to set you on a path of discovery, this section has a dash more NLP magic. But in order for you to fully appreciate what I am sharing with you in this guidebook, you need to know NLP's guiding principles or assumptions, which are called the NLP Presuppositions.

These presuppositions are assumed to be true – not because they are - but because regardless of what someone says, we judge behaviour. They are for structuring our perception when we deal with people, in this case our prospects. So, were you to choose to believe and adopt them, they would give you a much greater freedom of choice and opportunity and make a difference in achieving successful results. They will lead to a profound way of creating change for yourself. This I say hand on heart, and from personal experience.

Some of these principles you may recognize, since I have mentioned a few of them previously.

Presuppositions of NLP[3]	An explanation of them
Respect the other person's model of the world	People create their own experiences. The map (thoughts and feelings) is not the territory (reality). We respond to our maps rather than directly to the world. Our thoughts do change how we feel and, therefore, how we experience our world. It is easier to change our perception than change the world.
The meaning of your communication is the response you get	Notice the reaction to your communication. Alter it accordingly - be flexible. Your prospect may have heard something different to what you meant. You and your prospect are 100% responsible for the communication. You cannot NOT communicate; you are always communicating: - 93% of communication is outside conscious awareness - - 55% in non-verbal behaviour and 38% tonality - Your prospect will hear the words, but picks up other clues through your smiling (or not) and voice tone - Your body, whether in a state of comfort or discomfort, will impact on how you sound, what you say and the way you say it. Make sure you are in a comfortable position and space to make your telesales calls
The words we use are NOT the event or the item they represent	Words count for only 7% of the communication. All meaning is context dependent. Therefore, words require context for meaning.

---

[3] "The NLP Practitioner Manual", by Tad James and Advanced Neuro Dynamics, used with kind permission.

Perfecting The Art Of Telesales *Spiced With The Magic Of Neuro-Linguistic Programming*

The mind and body affect each other	The state of your mind affects the state of your body because they are part of the same system.
	Thoughts provoke feelings, which in turn affects posture, breathing, muscle tension, speech, etc. and this in turn affects thoughts - and the cycle goes around.
	Pay attention to the state of your mind and the state of your body before you start making your calls.
The most important information about a person is that person's behaviour	All behaviour has positive intention, although it is not always easy to see or hear.
	Even the prospect's most thoughtless behaviour has a positive purpose at the outset. At the time you call, if he is emotional and rude and slams down the phone, he started out with a positive intention.
	His behaviour is inappropriate, but is not personal. So, rather than condemning his actions, learn to separate intention from behaviour so you will think positively about him next time you call.
	He is thinking of other things when he answers a call, as a result he is not always in the right frame of mind or the right situation to take a call.
	Consider this, when the telephone rings at home we interrupt any number of domestic tasks to answer it:
	- leap out of a nice warm bath - stop eating our dinner - stop reading to our children
	We even have voice-mail or answering machines to take our calls.
	So out of habit, your prospect does the same: he interrupts his work task to answer your call. He is ill-prepared to take your call that is all.

Perfecting The Art Of Telesales *Spiced With The Magic Of Neuro-Linguistic Programming*

Behaviour is geared for adaptation, and the present behaviour is the best choice available	Every one of us has our unique way of being. We are trying to adapt to situations, and situations can change from moment to moment. We are the sum total of our experiences to date. From these experiences we make all our choices, until we learn new and better ways of doing things. This is also true for your prospect. People work perfectly. Our specific thoughts and emotions consistently produce specific results in our actions (behaviour). We may be happy or unhappy about those results, but if we repeat the same thoughts and provoke the same emotions it will produce the same behaviour; therefore, our processes (patterns of thinking and behaving) work perfectly – people work perfectly. This presupposition also means that people are doing the best they can with the knowledge skill and experience they have at this moment in time; meaning, given that premise, that people work perfectly. This is not, repeat not, about whether people are performing a job or task perfectly based on your judgement, but they are doing the best they can with the resources they have available to them. This presupposition implies forgiveness. You will, more often than not, need to forgive your prospect's behaviour.
A person's behaviour is not who they are	You are more than your behaviour, aren't you? Accept the person, change behaviour.

People have all the ability they need to succeed	There are no unresourceful people only unresourceful states. Thoughts, feelings of strength, courage, confidence, our inner voice of conviction, etc. are all resources we can draw on when we need them. We have endless resources and these develop with different experiences as we make our way through life. There are no limitations, other than those you choose to make for yourself.
You are in charge of your mind and therefore your results	You always have choice of thought. When you think differently you experience differently.
The system (person) with the most flexibility of behaviour will control the system	Develop flexibility of behaviour - you will control the telesales conversation.
There is no failure, only feedback	We each have our own learning style. You can never fail. Again, it means if you pay attention to the feedback (which comes in a variety of ways, the prospect says something, your boss, your spouse or your partner point to a better way of doing something, you start to notice things for yourself) and **make changes** you will more likely succeed, or be nearer to gaining what you want. When you repeat the same patterns you achieve the same outcomes. If you want something to be different – do something different. You have many choices.
Resistance in a client is a sign of a lack or rapport	There are no resistant prospects and customers, only inflexible telephone sales people. Be flexible and create more rapport.

NLP is at the heart of effective communication and change. It is a process for modeling patterns of thoughts, feelings and actions (behaviour).
I trust it will encourage you to make it a lifetime study for your holistic well-being.

Meaningful communication

"I know you believe you understand what you think I said.
However, I am not sure whether you realize that what you heard, is not what I meant"

Source: Anon.

1. Communication is the sum of everything you need to do in order to exchange ideas, feelings, attitudes and any other information between yourself and other people, groups and organizations.

2. The communication may be said to be effective when it evokes a positive response, establishing that the purpose of your communication has been achieved.

3. A good deal of face-to-face communication fails to achieve its aims because not enough thought has been given to its:

   - Preparation
   - Process and structure
   - Content and context
     Or delivery

4. The meaning of your communication is the response you elicit!

5. The meaning of your communication comprises[4]:

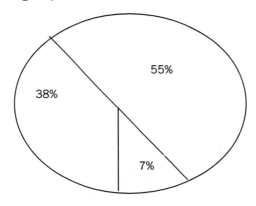

55% body language – non-verbal communication (posture, breathing, facial expression and gestures)

38% Tone – verbal behaviour (tone of voice and its unique quality, pitch, pace, volume, rhythm)

7% words- the content (the utterances that make up what we call our language – language triggers, common experiences, content chunks)

6. When using the telephone all the same applies, and remember there is even less feedback because of the lack of body language.

---

[4] "Kinesics and Communication", Robert Birdwhistle, University of Pennsylvania, 1970

Perfecting The Art Of Telesales *Spiced With The Magic Of Neuro-Linguistic Programming*

Example of the human communication process

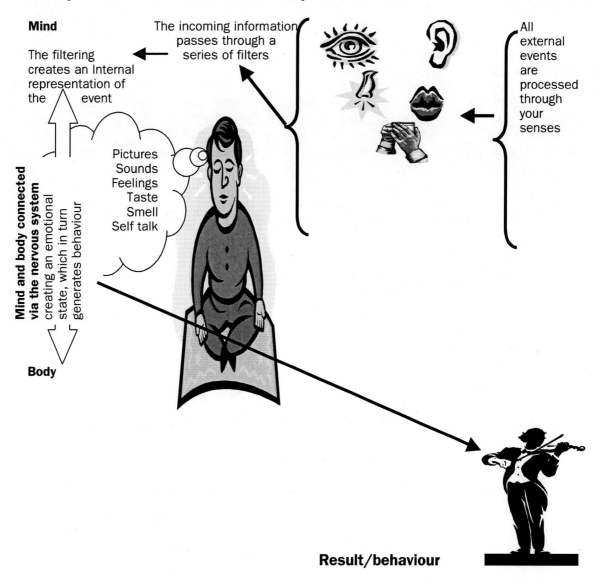

Mind

The incoming information passes through a series of filters

The filtering creates an Internal representation of the event

Pictures
Sounds
Feelings
Taste
Smell
Self talk

All external events are processed through your senses

Mind and body connected via the nervous system
creating an emotional state, which in turn generates behaviour

Body

Result/behaviour

I explained on **page 3** that superstar athletes use the technique of visualization, i.e. seeing themselves successfully performing the tasks in their mind before actualizing the tasks. So if you want to be a peak performer and successful communicator then this will be a useful technique for you to know.

NLP will help you to focus you on being more conscious of using the power of your mind, and the way it is programmed, to bring about your success.

In my example above I am simply demonstrating two things: (1) how the process of behaviour (positive or negative) is generated, and showing that there is filtering we all use to bring it about; and (2) the technique of visualization (used for generating a desired positive result by consciously using the programming available to us) brings about greater success. This also highlights that your success, or not, is totally self-determined by how you use the power of the programming in your mind.

Perfecting The Art Of Telesales *Spiced With The Magic Of Neuro-Linguistic Programming*

You want to become a successful telesales person!

Realize, learn about and then use the programming in your mind to shape the successful achievement of any goal you set yourself.

Of course, there is more to it than just knowing that the programming exists, and that the visualization helps, so later in this section we focus on a structured format for 'gaining what you want' (**see pp. 227-231.**)

We all process information through the same types of filters but our preference as to which we use, and our internal representations (IRs), are completely unique, which is why we have to respect other people's model of the world, and no two people have the same experience – ever.

Some of the filters we use are:

- Deletion
- Distortion
- Generalization
- Time/when
- Space/where
- Matter/what
- Energy/how

- Language
- Memories
- Decisions
- Meta programs
- Values & beliefs
- Attitudes

As we process the event, we delete, distort and generalize the information that comes in, according to several elements that filter our perception.

Deletion

Deletion occurs when we selectively pay attention to certain aspects of our experience and not others. Without deletion, we would be faced with too much incoming information to handle with our conscious mind. It is reported that the conscious mind can only handle as many as nine or as few as five items of information at any given time, and if we do not actively delete information, we would end up a little crazy.

Our ability to delete is essential to our sanity and survival.

Example:

I love Paris in the
the Springtime

Do you know the the way to
San Jose?

He's got the the whole world
in his hands

In order to make sense of what you see, you need to delete that which doesn't make sense, the extra 'the', which often isn't noticed. Did you notice it?

Distortion

Distortion occurs when we make shifts in our experience of the incoming sensory data by altering our perception. The purpose of distortion is to make sense of what we are seeing based on our current experience. An example: If you have ever moved home, you visit an empty house or flat, and then imagine your furniture placed in the rooms. This is distortion, an ability to create in your mind what is not there. Distortion makes it possible for you to dream, fantasize, be creative, and make future plans.

Generalization

A process of helping our learning, by taking information we have and drawing global conclusions. Many new behaviours are made up from previous experiences, which are similar to the new behaviour, and because of this we are relieved of the need to learn the new behaviour from the beginning. This may explain how we are able to learn as rapidly as we do.

This also perhaps goes some way to answer the question "when two people have the same stimulus, why don't they have the same response?" The answer is because we use deletion, distortion, and generalization.

This is why in telephone selling we cannot use the same presentation to each and every prospect. They each have a unique model of the world.

We delete, distort and generalize information that comes in via our senses based on one of five filters. The filters are: Meta-programs, belief systems, values, decisions and memories.

Before continuing, it is important to restate that humans are infinitely flexible. This information on filtering changes within different contexts of your life. You are never all one way, all the time. No one ever is.

Meta programs

The how and why we do things, and we have individual preferences that make sense to us. These Meta Programs change with context, time and emotional state.

One important point about Meta-Programs: they are not good or bad, they are just the way someone deletes information, and the way we make up our model of the world. They are filters embedded in our unconscious and affect what we:

- Notice – don't notice
- Like – don't like

How we:

- Make decisions
- Respond to stress
- Think
- Prefer to work

Values

Values are our attractions or repulsions in life. They are essentially a deep, unconscious belief system about what is important and what is good or bad to us. Values too change with context. They are how we decide whether our actions are good or bad, or right or wrong, and how we feel about our actions.
Values are what motivate us, and are arranged in a hierarchy with the most important one typically being at the top and lesser ones below that. If you change the order of your values you will be motivated differently.

Beliefs

Beliefs are generalizations about how the world is, and either create or deny personal power to us. So, beliefs are essentially our on/off switch for our ability to do anything in the world. Henry Ford said "If you believe you can or you can't, you're right."

Some of our beliefs we inherit through our parents, teachers, various situations we have been exposed to, and at certain periods in our lives, they have been serving us. However, as an adult you may find that some of your beliefs, for example, are your mother's/father's and served you as a child but no longer do. So be sure your beliefs are yours, pay attention when you hear yourself saying "I believe such and such..." make sure you do. The beliefs that are serving you - keep them; those that need to be eliminated or changed to empower you - make sure you change them.

- What do you believe about yourself?

- What do you need to believe about yourself to be excellent at telesales?

Perfecting The Art Of Telesales *Spiced With The Magic Of Neuro-Linguistic Programming*

Memories

In the context of telesales, I would say that memories, usually unresourceful memories, play a large part in preventing people making successful telephone sales calls. Poor telesales experiences and rejection are a challenge to ignore, but you can decide to be excellent at telephone sales and believe that you are...and so it will be.

Pay attention to the poor memories as you experience them, and note down the trigger. Then either change the situation or change the way you think about it.

Current emotional state:

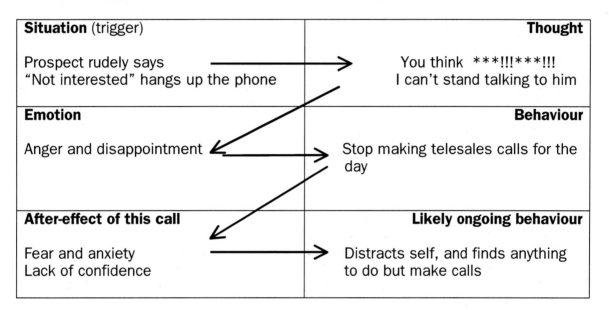

Situation (trigger)	**Thought**
Prospect rudely says "Not interested" hangs up the phone	You think ***!!!***!!! I can't stand talking to him
Emotion	**Behaviour**
Anger and disappointment	Stop making telesales calls for the day
After-effect of this call	**Likely ongoing behaviour**
Fear and anxiety Lack of confidence	Distracts self, and finds anything to do but make calls

New emotional state:

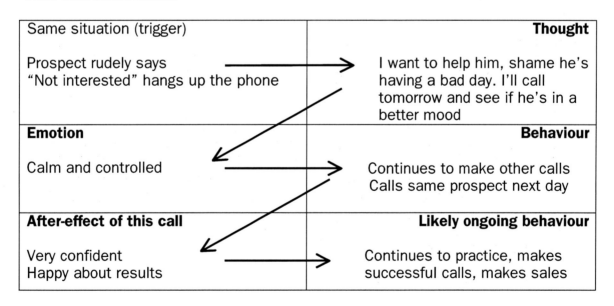

Same situation (trigger)	**Thought**
Prospect rudely says "Not interested" hangs up the phone	I want to help him, shame he's having a bad day. I'll call tomorrow and see if he's in a better mood
Emotion	**Behaviour**
Calm and controlled	Continues to make other calls Calls same prospect next day
After-effect of this call	**Likely ongoing behaviour**
Very confident Happy about results	Continues to practice, makes successful calls, makes sales

Perfecting The Art Of Telesales Spiced With The Magic Of Neuro-Linguistic Programming

Decisions

Decisions are related to memories. Decisions may create beliefs, or may just affect our perceptions through time. The problem with many decisions is that they were made either unconsciously or at a very early age, and are forgotten, and because we do not re evaluate them they often affect our life in ways we had not intended. Just decide to make things different, be open to change.
In telesales if you have decided that it is boring and difficult to do cold calling and prospecting, then it will be so. Alternatively you can decide it's easy, enjoyable and fun and if you don't decide it is easy, enjoyable and fun, be surprised to find you get results either way.

Attitude

An attitude is a collection of beliefs and values around a given subject - telephone selling. So what you value about following this profession has more to do with your success than perhaps you realized. If your attitude towards telephone selling is poor, then the likelihood of your making a success of it will be limited. You need to be conscious of your attitude towards telephone selling. If it is positive and you tell yourself and others "I love it, it's a great profession" you will be very successful.

Time/when; space/where; matter/what; energy/how; and Language.

When you do the calling, where you are, what you are focusing on, how you are feeling, how often you will do the calling, what you are saying to yourself about it, are crucial to the success of the task. As is, what you specifically do and the language you use in a telesales call.

In summary, these filters, along with others will determine your internal representation of an event that is occurring – even one that is happening to you right now. Your internal world puts you in a certain emotional state, and creates a certain physiology. The emotional state in which you find yourself will determine your behaviour.

<u>The <u>emotional</u> <u>state</u> <u>you</u> <u>are</u> <u>in</u> is the <u>emotional</u> <u>state</u> <u>you</u> <u>give.</u></u>

Be aware of your emotional state when making telesales calls. Successful, motivated happy states will generate (eventually) the same emotional state in your prospect.

Your every experience is something that you literally 'make up' inside your head.

'Make up' your telephone selling success. See yourself successful, hear yourself being successful, feel that success, and talk to yourself positively about it.

Building rapport

A key to success in most environments is the ability to get on with others.

This ability is useful whenever you interact with people.

However, it is crucial where the success of your work depends fully on being able to negotiate with and motivate others.

Since the meaning of communication is visual and mostly non-verbal, and effective communication is best achieved through face-to-face interaction, this provides you with a challenge in telephone selling.

Firstly, remember the **meaning** of communication is said to comprise

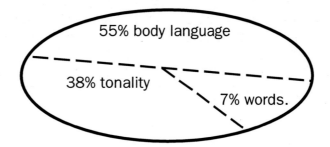

highlighting that 93% of the meaning of communication is outside your conscious awareness, and in order to fully communicate meaning there is dependency upon all three.

This means you have to compensate for the lack of body language, because before you can expect to achieve any level of agreement in a sale you have to establish rapport.

In some cases you may find it simple and natural to develop rapport with your prospect, so much so you probably don't notice it happening. In other cases you will have to work at it, and occasionally you may call prospects you feel uncomfortable but with whom you will have to build rapport and build good working relationships.

This is where the behaviours identified as **'rapport building'** are extremely useful.

Rapport is built through body language, words and tonality.

Rapport is the process of responsiveness, without necessarily liking.

When people are alike, they like each other. In telephone selling, creating rapport (whether or not you like your prospect) is necessary in order to have him buy from you.

Generally, people only buy from people they like.

The key process in rapport building is **'matching'**.

People who are in rapport tend to match or copy each other in a number of ways. You might say that we like and feel at ease with people who are like us.

If you watch people who are getting on well together, you will find that they tend to adopt similar body postures. They match physiology. They may for example:

- Sit in a similar manner
- Cross or uncross arms or legs at the same time
- Or use similar gestures and facial expressions

The benefits of becoming aware of the actions you can take to build rapport are two-fold:

1. With practice you develop skills available at a conscious level of competence, i.e. you can know if ever rapport is lost, and choose when to increase it

2. You also develop an unconscious level of competence, thus gaining a 'natural' ability to communicate and have a greater influence with your prospects or customers

The major elements of rapport are:

- Physiology - body posture and movement

- Voice – it's characteristics

- Language and thinking styles, and choice of words

- Beliefs and values – what prospects hold as important and true for them in their business world

- Experience – finding common experiences and associations

Body posture and movement is often thought of as unimportant when you are on the telephone. In point of fact it is essential to the overall atmosphere of the call. So you have to be more mindful of what body posture is, and why you should pay attention to and compensate for it when you are on the telephone.

It is true to say the more you can match prospect's behaviour, the deeper the rapport is likely to be.

Perfecting The Art Of Telesales *Spiced With The Magic Of Neuro-Linguistic Programming*

In a **face-to-face sales** situation you would probably behave in the following ways:

Physiology - body posture

- Sitting upright, leaning slightly forward having an active body state
- Posture being open and accepting is more engaging to the communication - also most people prefer to listen with their head slightly cocked to one side

Whilst avoiding communication barriers such as

- Folding arms, propping up head on your hand
- Crossing your legs, and the way in which you cross them will mean different things in different cultures
- Sitting back in the chair looking too relaxed

Eye contact

- It is thought that effective communicators show ease with each other when they achieve eye contact for up to 80% of the conversation
- Eye contact of course should be varied so that you do not stare. You must alternate between business and social gaze
- Similarly, avoid looking away for too long whilst you write notes

Gestures

- Open hand gestures; sitting with uncrossed arms, smiling
- Nodding when actively listening shows the prospect your understanding or interest
- Gestures that assist in reaching agreement, broadening the scope of discussion and increasing the exchange of information
- Avoiding the use of over dominant gestures, like pointing

Distance

- It is important to maintain distance to allow each party to feel relaxed
- Whilst there is evidence to suggest that the relationship improves with the action of coming closer, you would find a balance to build trust without invading the prospect's personal space

Perfecting The Art Of Telesales Spiced With The Magic Of Neuro-Linguistic Programming

So on **the telephone**, as your prospect cannot see you, it will be as well to **'act as if'** he could. This will help build and maintain rapport.

In point of fact as you pay attention to yourself whilst you are on the phone you will be amazed how many postures, gestures, eye movements and physical movements you make.

You may find yourself for example:

- Picturing what the prospect looks like
- Your body is in an active state, upright
- You are taking notes
- Actively listening with head tilted to one side
- You may discover that you have a preference for which ear you use when making your calls; i.e. you may find you are able to listen more intently with one ear more than the other
- You gesture with your hands when you are endeavouring to make a point
- You may periodically get up and walk around or pace whilst you are speaking – thus keeping your energy high, or helping you to feel more confident and determined (although it is not easy to take notes whilst pacing around!)

All this is observable behaviour - all of it increasing or decreasing rapport!
When you feel comfortable with the prospect - this is rapport.
When you feel ill at ease, for example, butterflies in your stomach or any anxiety in the chest, you are no longer in rapport. These feelings can be anywhere in the body. Pay attention to where you feel them, they will be unique to you.

Many of the movements you make unconsciously are to put you back into rapport, however, you may have never noticed until now. So pay attention.

You have many clues to help you in your endeavours for telephone selling, for gaining and maintaining rapport – be aware and sensitive to what is going on in the call.

A sensitive telesales person, will be 'actively listening' for and 'sensing' harmony between the intellectual verbal message and the clusters of non-verbal communication (which you cannot see but can sense).

When you sense discord between the words and hidden body language, you will ask yourself why? What must I do to restore rapport, trust and rebuild the relationship? This super 'sense' needs to be developed on the telephone and is fundamental to telephone selling success.

So, even during telephone selling it is likely you are matching your prospect's body movements. You cannot see this happening but you can sense it, and how important it is to the success of your call.

Perfecting The Art Of Telesales *Spiced With The Magic Of Neuro-Linguistic Programming*

What will have the greatest impact in telephone selling is matching your prospect's voice and voice patterns:

Volume	Does he speak loudly or softly?
Tempo	How fast or slow does he speak?
Rhythm	Is there a melody to his sentence? Or is his pattern clipped or pronounced in some way?
Pitch	High or low?
Timbre	What unique qualities do you hear in his voice?
Phrases	Is he using characteristic sayings, or regional colloquialisms?

This is **'auditory matching'** and whilst learning to use it to build and maintain rapport please remember to be subtle and respectful. Begin by matching one thing and then add in others. Listen, and as you hear all the different aspects of his voice, change your own voice only as quickly as is natural to the flow of the conversation:

- **Tone:** Do a temperature check. His mood is reflected in his tonality, so respect and fall in with the prospect's mind-set, and if necessary lead him to a happier frame of mind by staying upbeat, positive and enthusiastic. If he is in a poor state, never stay in his state with him, if you cannot lead him to a more positive frame of mind, it will be as well to close the call and ring him back another time. He might just cheer up because you are sensitive to his mood and he will make more effort to be sociable. Remember he also matches your behaviour!

- **Words:** Listen for the sensory-based words (**see pp. 145-157, 170-173**), write down key things he says and in the way he says them and repeat them back. Meaning, if he says he wants "efficiency" you say "we can do...which will give you the 'efficiency' you require". As opposed to you saying 'efficient' when he said 'efficiency'. There will be more emotional charge on the word for him if you use exactly the same one he used. So listen for content chunks, common words and phrases.

Creating rapport using the voice only requires that you focus on **what you say and the way you say it.**

Tonality is more influential than the words, so for telephone selling you need to **'voice match'** to build rapport, whilst still paying attention to your body posture. In summary:

- You actively listen, and make notes of his key phrases or key words and use these when you make your response.

- You also match his tone, rate of the speech, pitch and volume.

- Avoid mimicking an accent, if you do this unconsciously and well, your prospect would never notice. If you do it, and poorly, the prospect will possibly take offence.

- Volume and speed you will find easy to match. You may find that much of this happens automatically as you have a natural desire to be in rapport – humans are social animals after all.

Understanding the language of the senses

In telephone selling you have to love conversation, and enjoy listening to the way your prospect speaks. You will find it interesting to discover that listening to the types of language he uses, can tell you a lot about his thinking styles and preferences. To match your prospect's thinking styles is a powerful way of developing deep rapport.

Thinking is a complex function, but there are some clues to help you build rapport. There are four primary distinctions to be made in types of thinking: these are indicated by the use of visual, auditory and feeling triggers in language.

Visual: Thinking in pictures

If he thinks in a visual way he will tend to use language that contains visual words and phrases. For example "*I get the picture*", "*Let's try to put this into perspective*". So if you want to build rapport with him you might begin by saying you "*See his point of view*". Or "*See things more clearly now*", this will encourage him to "*View things your way*".

Auditory tonal: Thinking in sounds

Similarly, auditory thinking may be indicated by auditory words and phrases e.g. "*I hear what you say*", "*Sounds good to me*". When you listen to the kinds of words he says in his sentences and match them, he realizes that you "*Talk the same language*" and what you say "*Rings true*" for him too.

Feeling: Represent thoughts as feelings

If your prospect has to access a feeling (and the idea of movement he also finds appealing) he will tend to use 'feeling' type language and words related to touch. For example "*We are getting to grips with the problem now*" or "*Things are moving along smoothly and comfortably*".

When you want to get in touch with him you could get a feel for the type of words he prefers to use. If you then use similar language you may notice how things between you are "*Going along nicely*".

Auditory digital: Thinking in words and self-talks

This kind of thinking is indicated by words and phrases e.g. "*That makes sense*", "*If you can give me the information in a logical order*". When you listen to the kind of words he says in his sentences and match them, he realizes that you "*Follow the same train of thought*" and what you say "*Is logical*" for him too.

You are aware that these thinking styles are known as internal representation systems (IRs) and they are the way in which people represent the world to themselves inside their mind.

However, you may not have considered until now how much effort goes into sensory based communication and thinking. Consider now...

As you are taking this information in, you are processing it through the five senses (assuming you have all five). Sight, hearing, feeling, taste, smell, you also have an internal dialogue – i.e. you talk to yourself.

This processing goes through a series of other filters as previously mentioned. Not all the filters that we use are mentioned in this guidebook but are comprehensively explained in other NLP books (**see p. 243.**)

You are making up your model of your world and how you experience it through the five senses, and your thinking is a mixture of them.

Think of 'petrol'. What comes to your mind? May be you:

- Imagined a petrol station, with the brand colours indicating which oil company
- Saw a car at a petrol pump. Was it your car? Were you in the picture?
- Heard the sound of the petrol pumping, the clicking sound of the rising price and volume indicators ticking over as the tank fills
- Smelled petrol
- Were you having a conversation with yourself about the price of petrol

It is interesting what comes to mind isn't it?

Test this out with a group of your friends or colleagues. Just ask them, "if I say 'petrol' what comes to mind?" Take the first answers they give. What you will notice is what they generate inside their head, and all of them will have a completely different experience and answer.

Even as you read through this guidebook, I have no idea what you are seeing, hearing, feeling, thinking and whether you are making sense of anything I have written so far. What I know is, how important it is to engage all the senses to enhance and convey understanding of the communication to all readers. The same is true when you are selling.

You see, none of us communicate in the same way (and none of us buy for the same reason either). This is because some of us have a preference for thinking in:

- Pictures - to see how something looks to us before we buy

- Sounds - we may like the sound of what is said about a product or service

- Feelings - we need to be relaxed and comfortable about the purchase we are about to make

- Words and talking to yourself (internal dialogue - to make sense of a product or service before we consider a purchase

Some of us use a combination of all of these, or sometimes only one or two, to make up our model of the world. So for example we may have to see and feel something in order to decide.

It is important to emphasize that this style of thinking does not just relate to buying but applies in all contexts of our lives. And the styles of thinking can and often do change with context. You are infinitely flexible. There is no right or wrong way, it is just the way we represent the world to ourselves.

What is important for you to realize is, the more senses you can engage, the higher the quality of the information given and received, the greater the retention the prospect has of your conversation.

When you actively listen you will start to notice that you, and your prospect, use sensory-based words to describe your experience. Pay attention, you can recognize and match the words used by him, and then you will be really speaking his language.

If you are already in the habit of noting down and repeating back information that your prospect says, in the way he says it, you may find you already speak his language. This is a well-known sales technique, and now you understand the real power behind it and you can use it more consciously.

The sensory-based words we all use to make up our model of the world are known as our 'language triggers'.

Language trigger examples

A prospect that has a **visual preference** has a tendency to the following:

- Memorizes by seeing pictures and is less distracted by noise

- Often has trouble remembering long verbal instructions, and is bored by them so his mind tends to wander

- Is interested in how a product/service looks

Since you cannot show him something on the telephone unless you have web based product/information that you can direct him too; or you have sent him something to view, you can notice and match his preference using visual language.

You can also notice that he tends to speak at a fast pace. So you can match his pace and words.

He will tend to use these kinds of:

Words	Phrases
- View	"Get a perspective on"
- Show	"I need to view"
- Dawn	"Beyond a shadow of a doubt"
- Reveal	"It's crystal clear"
- Clear	"Let me examine"
- Foggy	"It appears to me"
- Focused	"I need a snapshot of"
- Hazy	"I will be showing this to my group, and their views will influence my final decision"
- Imagine	

Telephone selling to visually orientated prospect

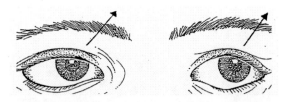

You cannot see this happening, when you use visual words, your prospect will look up and to his left (your right if you were looking at him) when seeing a picture of something he has seen before – a clear image from his memory bank.

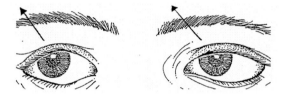

When he looks up and over to his right (your left if you were looking at him), he is imaging something he has never seen. Your product or service in his business.

So remember:

-    A picture paints a thousand words to him

-    He would ordinarily like to see charts, graphs, photos, and slides. Or have you draw images on a whiteboard

-    Since you are not with him, direct him to look at certain pages in your brochure, or on your website. Or send him relevant information that shows pictures. Guide him to the appropriate places to look. (The danger of having him look at something whilst on the telephone is that he may become totally distracted by it, so keep control of what he is to look at. Direct him and ask him questions to keep him involved in the conversation.)

-    Trialing the product may be important to him

-    Use words to paint vivid pictures

When you want your prospect to think visually, glance upwards (this is how we access visual information), it may just be that your prospect at the other end of the phone may follow your lead, and match your behaviour - you are in rapport; even when you cannot see him it does not mean he is not doing what you are doing and use statements like:

- "Does that look good to you?"

- "Let me show you, if you look at page...you will see..."

- "I want you to imagine yourself using this..."

- "Is that clear to you?"

Closing on the phone for the visual:

- Have him sketch down ideas (if you can) of the benefits of what you are offering

- Go through images as you get him to agree to see how it will benefit him

- If your prospect says **"I cannot see what you are saying"**. Then he is telling you that you have not created enough of a visual image for him to understand your message and be convinced. You will need to build more rapport and give information using visual language

Remember too 'dress for success'.

Prospects judge you by your professionalism, and this is particularly true of some visuals, who may judge the appearance of documents you send.

The way you present information in a letter or email. Visual impact is important to him. So dress everything up to create the impression you need to have him say yes – "I like what I see".

You may also be the kind of person who needs to 'dress up' to make telephone sales calls. For some, looking and feeling good makes a difference to their confidence and motivation level. Even when the prospect cannot see you, he can imagine and hear how you feel!

If your prospect processes **through his feelings**, then he may have a tendency to process the information in the following ways.

Clues for those accessing feelings  are:

- His talk is often very slow and breathy. In fact his rate of speech can be sometimes extremely irritating if you are a fast pace speaker/listener

- However, it is not that this prospect is slow witted. He just accesses and processes information at a slower pace

- **It will be imperative that you match his pace** and **never rush him**; otherwise he will switch off and have you repeat information more than once

- He will also respond to physical rewards and touching

- He memorizes by doing or walking through something

- He will be interested in a product/service that "feels right" or gives him a "gut feeling"

You have to make an effort to give him the right feel about what you are saying over the telephone. He will tend to use these kinds of:

Words	**Phrases**
- Feel	"I need to get a handle on this"
- Touch	"It all boils down to"
- Grasp	"If I can pull the right strings I will"
- Get hold of	"You need to get in touch with"
- Catch on	"We always need hands on approach in this department"
- Tap into	"I'll touch base with...and find out how he feels about it"
- Make contact	

Perfecting The Art Of Telesales Spiced With The Magic Of Neuro-Linguistic Programming

Telephone selling to a feeling orientated prospect

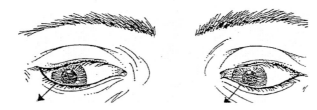

You cannot see this happening, when you use feeling words your prospect will look down and to his right (your left if you were looking at him) when accessing his emotions.

So, (look down and to the left so you access a positive feeling – he may do the same, even though you cannot see this) make your pace, slow, warm and sincere.

Use physical action and emotional words:

- "How do you feel about the proposal?"

- "I need to get a handle on your exact requirements"

- "Once you are comfortable with these changes, we can move on to installing the product"

Ideally, this type of prospect needs 'contact'. As this is not possible over the phone, you will need to get him more physically involved with the product. Have him enter something into his computer, i.e. touching the keys or moving through a presentation. Or send him something he can hold, feel the finish of, as this will heighten and fulfil his tactile need.

This prospect also needs to be physically comfortable when taking your call, so it is imperative to pay attention to how he answers the telephone. If he sounds distracted or distressed, check the convenience to continue with the conversation. If he is not comfortable he will ignore a lot of what you say.

Closing on the phone for the feeling prospect

As he would ideally like a handshake, make sure you access a positive feeling, it will make you sound more sincere. Say for example:

- "You agree that this feels right for you, great, I feel very good about it too."

- "You will feel very contented and proud to own one of these"

- If this prospect says **"I cannot grasp your meaning"**. This means this prospect needs more feeling based words to have him feel good about what you are offering.

Perfecting The Art Of Telesales *Spiced With The Magic Of Neuro-Linguistic Programming*

Those who have an **auditory tonal preference**

- This prospect will be easily distracted by noise (so if there is background noise in your office, or his, then his concentration may waiver)

- He can repeat things back to you easily, he learns by listening

- Tone of voice and words used are important

- This prospect is the easiest to deal with, as he too, likes to talk on the telephone

However, his voice can be monotone, which can be a challenge for you to listen to over a long period of time. His pace is fast but not as fast as those who process visually.

Telephone selling to an auditory tonal oriented prospect

You cannot see this happening, when you use your tone and words to match your prospect he will look horizontally to the left (your right if you were looking at him) when constructing new sounds he has not heard before.

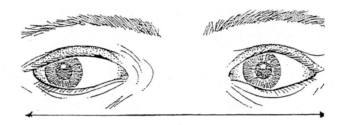

He looks horizontally to the right (your left if you were looking at him) when remembering sounds or voices he has heard before.

It is key that you make your voice memorable to an auditory tonal prospect; he loves how things sound.

- He thinks in words and sounds so is strongly interested in what you will have to say about your product or service. Testimonials will also be important. It is likely he will ask for an opportunity to telephone for a reference

- He pays as much attention to how you say the words as to what you say

- He picks up any conflict (i.e. if what you are saying doesn't ring true!) very quickly and he will mentally switch off, particularly if he cannot believe what he is hearing

- He responds favourably or not to your tonality

Perfecting The Art Of Telesales *Spiced With The Magic Of Neuro-Linguistic Programming*

He will tend to use these kind of:

Words	Phrases
- Hear	"Do I need to amplify anything?"
- Listen	"Does that sound good to you?"
- Sound(s)	"I will have to tell…about this first"
- Rings true	"That is music to my ears"
- Tell me	"I am well informed about."
- Be heard	"What! A buying policy that's unheard of in our organization!"

Closing on the phone for the auditory tonal

- Send him something he can listen too, an audiocassette or CD, or have him look at a web-based presentation with sounds

- Talk him through the options whilst he is on the phone

- He likes to hear how it sounds. (You will possibly notice that as you take him through the information you are looking to your left, as this is how you remember information using your auditory sense)

- When this prospect says, **"It doesn't sound right to me"**, then build up the auditory-based words, and use your tone to heighten his experience and understanding

- This particular prospect may need frequent contact by phone, it means a great deal even when not a lot is said

Perfecting The Art Of Telesales *Spiced With The Magic Of Neuro-Linguistic Programming*

The final group has **a preference** for **auditory digital**  Information

- He will spend a fair amount of time talking to himself (internal dialogue)

- He memorizes by steps, procedures, and sequences

- He will want to know if your product/service "makes sense"

- He can also easily exhibit characteristics of the other preferences

- Words for him are important

- Digital language is invaluable for communicating ideas, concepts and even abstractions

- He loves words, and will often say 20 words when 5 will have done the job, and whatever he is given always has to make sense or be logical

- He often (not always) likes a lot of detail and follows logic easily

- Likes order of things, make lists, loves specifications

- He will tend to be medium-paced in his speech

He will tend to use these kinds of:

Words	**Phrases**
- Sense	"I need to think about this a lot more"
- Experience	"I like to understand every step of the way"
- Understand	
- Think	"When we have evaluated the process we will make a decision"
- Learn	
- Process	"I am conscious that...."
- Decide	"If we consider how to..."
- Consider	"I know when it makes sense we will be able to progress this to a logical conclusion"

Perfecting The Art Of Telesales *Spiced With The Magic Of Neuro-Linguistic Programming*

Telephone selling to an auditory digital orientated prospect

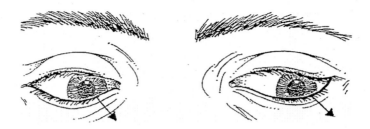

You cannot see this happening, when you use words your prospect will look down and to his left (your right if you were looking at him) when talking to himself – internal dialogue. This type of person likes lots of words. He is accustomed to and prefers words. Use greater detail about the features and relevant benefits of your products or service.

Use steps, processes, procedures, specifications or lists. Say:

- "I want you to get a good sense of what I am recommending. I will send a detailed proposal today"

- "I need to understand the criteria you have set; can you list it in order of priority"

- "If you can give me the list in order I will ensure we evaluate it that way for you"

- "I will send you our specification on this product so you can check it against your own"

- Use changes in your tonality, and pay attention to the words you choose to use

- This type of person picks up on what is said more than how – although he will notice and may react to your tonality

Closing on the phone for the auditory digital

- You can send this prospect visual information as long as it is ordered, logical, usually wordy, has steps, procedures, process and/or is easy for him to check a specification against his requirement

- He likes to contrast information – give him lists of things to consider

- Presentation will be important. He may look at any visuals you give him but verbal description with a list, sequential and logical detail will prove more convincing

- When talking with him, step him through the information

- Talk him through the options whilst he is on the phone and ask him to decide what is most sensible or logical to him

- It is likely that your eyes will be down and to the right as this is how logically based information is stored and where you hear your internal dialogue and make lists inside your head

- If this prospect says **"It doesn't make sense to me"**, build up rapport and the words in a procedural fashion

- Make it easy for him to hear and follow the logical order of what you are proposing

Note:

The preceding information is known as eye accessing. This information is given purely as a point of interest. It shows how, with the use of our natural eye movements, there are patterns to how we access different areas of our brain for our sensory information.

It is important to say that, in some people, these natural eye movements (which are used by us all) may be reversed. Meaning, they look in the opposite direction to the diagrams shown above. Since you cannot see them, you will not be able to test where they are looking.

What is important is that you pay attention to your prospect's **language** and, once you have recognized his preferred sensory communication channel, that you match that channel in the words and phrases that **you** use.

Language is the key to desired and positive results.

It is **imperative** that you understand that these communication channels and preferences change within different contexts of your life.

You are infinitely flexible as a human being. You continually learn, develop and change.

No one preference is any better than another. These preferences are the way we access and process information, and in different contexts we may use entirely difference preferences and use the sensory-based language associated with them.

As an example, I am highly auditory tonal and have digital preference probably through having done telephone selling for more than 20+ years. However, in the context of writing this guidebook I am endeavouring to employ all senses to increase the quality of my communication to you.

In the context of one of my hobbies, I have visual, auditory and feeling preferences for learning and replicating the patterns and rhythms required for Latin American dancing.

When you find that you easily and effortlessly move across all four communication channels (and you likely do, unconsciously), this means you are continually enhancing the quality of your communication with others.

The power of understanding this consciously is so you can pay attention to it and increase rapport and ensure motivation when you need to.

The last two elements of rapport

Beliefs and values

A deep level of rapport can be built relatively fast if you can match the belief and values of the prospect you are speaking with.

For example, you make several attempts reach this prospect but without success. When you finally make contact, he answers your call and makes some comment about not having much time to talk to you. So you match his belief about the value of his time as this will build an immediate empathy and respect, and will make him much more inclined to participate in the conversation.

You must actively listen for what he says as he takes your call. If for example he says, "Look I don't have much time to talk to you" you can say, "I see, (he said 'look' use -visual language) thanks, I appreciate your taking my call then Mr... how much time can you give me right now?" Wait for his time allowance. He says "I can let you have 5 minutes"

Now make a judgement on whether it is best to continue, and if it is not, arrange to call him when he has more time.

If you decide to continue:

- Repeat back what he says "I 'see', 5 minutes, thanks for this I will get straight to the point..." Now get to the point! You may find that once he is engaged in an interesting conversation he will carry on talking. If on the other hand he starts to sound distracted, acknowledge the time he has given you and offer to call back, send information, or whatever you deem is the best outcome at this point

- "Mr...I value the time you have given me this morning, but I am **conscious** you 'see' only 5 minutes available, so I don't want to take more of your time right now. How will it be if I call you back later in the week? Which day is best for you, Thursday or Friday afternoon?"

If you decide it is not appropriate to continue:

Say, "I 'see', 5 minutes, well I think it will be best if I call you another time when you can perhaps give me at least 15 minutes. Please can you 'look' in your diary and 'see' if you can fit me in sometime this week?" Wait for response, agree a date and time and close the call.

Experience

Again, this is a particularly useful form of matching when calling. When introducing yourself, engage his attention easily by referring to an experience that he may have had immediately prior to taking your call, or a current experience he is having now.

For example:

The person connecting your call to him tells you that he has just come back from a meeting.

You could say to him "I appreciate your time; I understand you have just come back from a meeting. Would you rather I give you a little more time and I will call you back later?" Get a time.

Or he says, as he picks up the phone "I have just this moment come into the office, I have been stuck in traffic for hours".

You could say, "Oh I am sorry to hear that, I know what that is like, isn't it frustrating sitting in traffic; do you want to take a few moments to get settled? I'll wait".

You will go up in the prospect's estimation by being sensitive to his current situation, and considerate of his time; it is likely he will just continue the conversation because you gave him the choice. This kind of behaviour builds rapport very quickly.

However, a common experience for the prospect is that you do not actively listen to what he says as he answers the call. He usually answers with a greeting like "Hello, Joe Bloggs here", but you respond with "Can I speak to Mr Bloggs please" or "Is that Mr Bloggs?". When this occurs it demonstrates to the prospect that you are not paying attention, and thus his precious time is already being wasted.

So, listen, and acknowledge what is said to you. If he answers the call using his name - greet him by using his name (and this applies to anyone answering your call not just the prospect) - if he gives you other useful information that gives you a clue to his state of mind/situation - use it - this is the 'experience' he is having at the moment you call him!

The indicators of rapport are:

- You will feel comfortable somewhere in your body (pay attention to where this feeling is. It is likely you feel uncomfortable there too when you are out of rapport)

- There may be a spontaneous positive comment from your prospect, "I'm glad you called" or "Haven't we spoken before?"

- You may feel a slight flushing in your face (like a mild form of embarrassment)

- You will create an ability to lead your prospect. Notice whether he begins to follow your voice qualities or your language (if you were sitting face to face he would follow your movements or gestures – this is known as leading)

When using leading as an influencing tool it is important to recognize its power, and as such be clear of your intention for influencing a situation:

- Why do you want to lead?
- Is the direction you are going in the prospect's best interest?

If you use leading at his expense, you might get away with it once, but remember you will likely damage any trust or relationship for future occasions.

You can match, pace and lead the prospect to postures or thinking that suggest more commitment. From these positions he is more likely to see things from your point of view, be comfortable moving to the next stage, think that your proposal is sensible, feasible and that it all sounds a perfect fit to his needs.

Unconscious motivation, working and decision-making traits

People have a unique model of the world based on the processing of information via their senses and through a variety of unconscious filters.

Some of this filtering and processing also applies to how people are motivated and how they make decisions. Your being aware of their presence and what they mean when telephone selling will help you achieve greater success from your calls.

Once you recognize the motivation, working and decision-making traits you will begin to build the language needed to ensure both you and your prospect are winners.

A prospect's true motivation is linked to his values, these being the label for the things that are important to him in a given context. Values are used to attract and maintain interest. As I have previously mentioned, he feels the emotions attached to the words he uses. For example, if he says, "I want higher 'productivity'" you match and use the same word. If, however, you say "So you want higher 'production'" this is a mis-match. You match by saying "So you want higher 'productivity' from ..." The emotional charge for him is on the word he uses.

So, these traits, unconscious to most of us until they are pointed out, provide information on how your prospect:

- triggers his motivation

- maintains his motivation, and how he works

For the purpose of explanation, these traits (which are shown on the following pages) are on what we will call a continuum. There is no right or wrong with these traits, it is just preference. It needs to be understood that a person can be at any point on the continuum, and the greater their ability to operate flexibly across the continuum, the higher the quality of their communication is likely to be to themselves and others. As you look at these traits you may start to notice your own preferences, and that in certain areas of your working life you easily use both, whereas in another you may use just one. In telephone selling it will be preferable that you develop an ability to use and respond appropriately to both.

You may be realizing now that you have a preference to use one trait more than another, i.e. operate at one end of the continuum, and this may prove to be detrimental to your sale because the same is true for your prospect. He can be anywhere on a continuum at any time, and may be operating at the opposite end of the continuum; he will thus behave differently in different buying contexts. You will need to be able to match his preferences to trigger and maintain his motivation.

These filters complement each other (and of course are mixed in with all other filtering) making up a complex and unique human being.

Perfecting The Art Of Telesales *Spiced With The Magic Of Neuro-Linguistic Programming*

You cannot put yourself or your prospect in a box of strict behaviours or personality types. No one behaves the same way all the time; different influences trigger different behaviours. People have behaviour that is not who they are. Please remember, humans are infinitely flexible.

I have been very selective in the filters I have chosen i.e. those most relevant to telephone selling.

You will only learn how to use these with concentrated effort, and practice. However, first you must build your confidence and skill in the basics of telephone selling, and then add the spice.

I know you would like to learn more about these filters known as Meta Programs[5], and the above information is based on a tool known as the Language and Behaviour Profile (LAB Profile)[6].

The following pages give examples of some of the motivation, working and decision making traits. The preference can be heard in the language used.

My simple examples are described as extremes of the traits for the purposes of explanation.

   = The continuum.

Remember he can, and you can be anywhere on this continuum at any time.

---

[5] "Words That Change Minds, Mastering the Language of Influence", Shelle Rose Charvet. Kendall/Hunt Publishing Company. Used with kind permission.

[6] Created by Rodger Bailey. The LAB Profile is a development based on specific tools from Neuro-Linguistic Programming (NLP).

Perfecting The Art Of Telesales *Spiced With The Magic Of Neuro-Linguistic Programming*

Motivation traits

How a prospect triggers his interest, or conversely what will de-motivate him

Trait	**Trait**
Proactive ⟵————————⟶	**Reactive**
Motivated by doing	Motivated by waiting or considering
Language to use:	**Language to use:**
Go for it. Just do it	Let us think about it Let's consider this
Toward ⟵————————⟶	**Away from**
Achieving goals	Solving or avoiding problems
Language to use:	**Language to use:**
Attain, obtain, have	Avoid, prevent, eliminate
Internal ⟵————————⟶	**External**
Decisions based on own internal standards	Decisions based on outside feedback
Language to use:	**Language to use:**
Only you can decide Its up to you	So and so thinks... Others will notice...
Options ⟵————————⟶	**Procedures**
Motivated by developing and creating systems. Has difficulty following set procedures	Motivated by following tried and tested set ways
Language to use:	**Language to use:**
Opportunities Lots of choice	Do it the right way This is tried and tested

Trait		**Trait**
Sameness	← →	**Sameness with exception**
Motivated by things staying the same		Motivated by situations evolving over time
Language to use:		**Language to use:**
The same as... Identical to...		More The same except... Gradual improvement
Difference	← →	**Sameness with exception and difference**
Motivated by change being constant and drastic		Motivated by evolution and revolution
Language to use:		**Language to use:**
New Totally different Unique		Use both sameness with exception and difference language

Working traits

The working traits are more about how your prospect will treat information, the types of tasks, and the environment in which he is most productive and how he is convinced and makes decisions.

As before these are continuums. No right or wrong, or better than, just the way he processes information – uniquely.

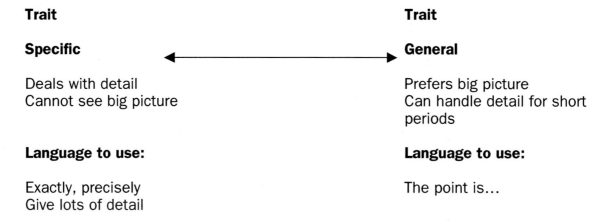

Trait	**Trait**
Specific	**General**
Deals with detail	Prefers big picture
Cannot see big picture	Can handle detail for short periods
Language to use:	**Language to use:**
Exactly, precisely	The point is…
Give lots of detail	

The moral of the specific and general traits highlight how important it is to match the right amount of information to the prospect's preference. There is little point in giving a lot of detail to someone who likes the big picture and vice versa, as he will mentally switch off.

In the prospect's language he will be indicating which he has a preference for.

If you cannot hear it, as it takes a lot of practise to start to recognize these patterns, just ask:

"Would you prefer me to send you an overview or a full information pack?"

His preference will be in his answer.

He may, of course, say both… which is OK too.

Convincers and decision-making traits

Another filter that is important to know for telephone selling is called the Convincer Channel, which identifies the preferred sense that has to be present in order for someone to be convinced.

A question you can ask to find his preference is:

"How do you know when a product/service is good?"

His response may be:

- I need to **see** some evidence
- I need to **hear** evidence, listen to feedback
- I need to **read** about it, reports, reference or testimonials
- I need to **do** something with the evidence

It will be important to match the sensory channel with your language.

The Convincer Channel is linked to the Convincer Mode, and identifies the number of times people have to see, hear, read or do to be convinced.

A question that will find out his preference is:

"How often does a supplier have to demonstrate competence to you before you are convinced?"

These two questions help you find the unconscious pattern the prospect is using, and gives you opportunity to match it to meet his convincer needs.

Decisions

Prospects fall into broad categories when making decisions.

Automatic decisions

In a work context
8% decide this way

This type of prospect is a telesales person's dream. Provided you meet his values and requirements in the right and preferred system (pictures, sounds, feelings, or it makes sense), he is convinced straight away and will make decisions easily and quickly.

Number of times

In a work context
52% decide this way

This prospect will need to have information presented a number of times. If he gives you a number, use his.

There is no rule about the number although the most common number is three times. So a recommendation would be to prepare three options: be prepared to call at least three times, or go over the information a number of times and perhaps in different ways.

Consistent

In a work context
15% decide this way

These prospects are never completely convinced. They need to re-evaluate every time and are always on the look out for more information.

You will need to say things like "Every time you use it"

Period of time

In a work context
25% decide this way

These prospects collect information over a period of time and say things like "I'll think it over", "Let me sleep on it",
"I'll see how I feel about it in a few days." Where this is a genuine trait, not a 'stall' to get you off the phone, he will need time to feel comfortable about making his decision.

Match his period of time. Do confirm that his decision will be made on that day, and that he will tell you what it is.

Adding more spice - the use of sensory-based Language

You were possibly not aware until now that you use sensory-based language and always have done. However using it more consciously will enhance your telesales calls. In telephone selling you appear to be using only the sense of hearing but you are linguistically engaging, or not, the prospect's other senses. Using sensory-based language more consciously will trigger a higher level of motivation to buy your product or service. Firstly a reminder:

Visual

Memorizes and learns by	Thinks	Rate of speech	And	An opportunity to	Is interested in a product or service that
Seeing pictures	In pictures. A picture paints a thousand words	Fast	Is bored by long rambling statements his mind will tend to wander.	Trial or see a demonstration of the product may be important.	"Looks right" or how a service will make him "Look good"

Auditory Tonal

Listening	In words and uses sound. Tone is very important. Has internal dialogue.	Medium paced and often monotone	Is strongly interested in what you will have to say and how. If it doesn't 'ring true' he will mentally switch off. He responds favourably or not to your tonality.	To have a telephone reference may be important.	"Sounds right"

Feelings

By doing	Slowly and links feelings. The emotion is Important.	Often very slow, and breathy	It is imperative that you match his pace and never rush him, otherwise he will switch off.	Operate or feel the finish of a product will fulfil his tactile need. An emotionally based testimonial about the service. Both may be important.	"Feels right" or gives him a "Gut feeling"

Auditory Digital

Steps, procedures and sequences	By self-talk. Abstract words used without a direct sensory link.	Medium pace	Words are important. Likes a lot of detail. Picks up on what is said more than how – although he will notice and may react to your tonality.	Contrast information, or have lists of sequential and logical detail. This will prove more convincing. He needs the logic.	"Makes sense"

Perfecting The Art Of Telesales *Spiced With The Magic Of Neuro-Linguistic Programming*

Examples of sensory based phrases

Visual	Auditory tonal	Feelings	Auditory digital
			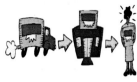

Visual

Eye to eye

Appears to me

Beyond a shadow of a doubt

Bird's eye view

Catch a glimpse of

In light of

Mind's eye

Paint a picture

Pretty as a picture

Sight for sore eyes

Take a peek

Dim view

Hazy idea

See to it

Auditory tonal

Give me your ear

Clear as a bell

Call on

Express yourself

Heard voices

Hidden messages

Hold your tongue

Loud and clear

Purrs like a kitten

Rings a bell

To tell the truth

Tune in/ tune out

In a manner of speaking

Voice an opinion

Feelings

Hand in hand

Boils down to

Cool calm collected

Treading on thin ice

Get a handle on

Get in touch with

Hang in there

Heated argument

Hold it

Hold on

Pull some strings

Sharp as a tack

Slipped my mind

Smooth operator

Under pressure

Auditory digital

Describe in detail the process

Give an account of

Pay attention to

State your purpose

Word for word

I need to think about

I like to understand every step of the way

When I have evaluated the process I will make a decision

I am conscious that...

If I consider how to...

I know when it makes sense I will be able to progress this to a logical conclusion

Perfecting The Art Of Telesales Spiced With The Magic Of Neuro-Linguistic Programming

Examples of phrases you can use in telephone selling for:

Visual

You could say:

"Does that look good to you?"

"Let me show you..."

"If you look at page...you will see..."

"I want you to imagine using this..."

"Is that clear to you?"

Or, if your prospect uses a combination of these triggers you could reply using the same mix:

"If you can **see** what I am **saying** then I will **call** your associate, and have him get in **touch** with the team working on the **details and specification**, is this ok with you?"

Auditory Tonal

"How does that sound to you?"

"Do I need to amplify anything?"

"I think I am in tune with what you have explained let me just tell you what I have understood..."

"Wouldn't you agree this is a **sound plan**, giving the team the chance **to view**, and **be comfortable** with the **criteria** before we start the project?"

Perfecting The Art Of Telesales Spiced With The Magic Of Neuro-Linguistic Programming

Feelings

You could say:

Or, if your prospect uses a combination of these triggers you could reply using the same mix:

"How do you feel about the proposal?"

"Are you comfortable with us making these changes?"

"I need to get a handle on your exact requirements"

"I know you are **under pressure**, so I will send **a detailed quote** for your consideration, and when you have **reviewed** it, we can **discuss** a start date. When shall I **call** you back, Friday or Monday?"

Auditory digital

"I want you to get a good sense of what I am recommending so I will send a detailed proposal today"

"I need to understand the criteria you have set, can you list it in order of priority?"

"If you can give me the list in order I will ensure we evaluate it that way for you".

"Given **the order** in which you need to deal with this project, I **think** you may find it helpful to see a **step by step** plan. The team can **view** the **process** and **discuss** it amongst themselves to **get a handle** on what needs to happen next – what do **you think**?"

Examples of tie down questions:

Visual   So when I **show** you beyond a **shadow** of a doubt a way in which you could (state benefit), you would at least want to **look** at it, wouldn't you?

Auditory Tonal   So when I give you proof of the strong **voices of opinion** in our favour of the ways in which you could (state benefit), you would at least want to **hear them**, wouldn't you?

Feelings   If I could **pull some strings** to have a sample of the product sent today (or if you will be **comfortable** with a reference about our service from one of our existing customers) that would give you a **feel** for how you will benefit, you would at least **get a handle** on it wouldn't you?

Auditory Digital When I send you **a specification**, which **details** your **precise** requirements in **logical order**, you will at least be able to **consider** our offer won't you?

The above examples I have made extreme to make the point of how sensory-based language can be used. Here are some simpler examples:

Visual   If I can **show** you a way in which you could (state benefit), you would want to **look** at it, wouldn't you?

Auditory Tonal   If I could **tell** you a way in which you could (state benefit), you would at least want to **hear** about it, wouldn't you?

Feelings   If there were a **concrete** way in which you could (state benefit), you would at least get a **feel** for it wouldn't you?

Auditory Digital If I detail your **precise requirements** with prices, and **list specifically** how you will benefit, you would be able to **decide** wouldn't you?

Make up some sensory based phrases of your own:

Visual	Auditory tonal	Feelings	Auditory digital

Tie- down questions:			
Visual	Auditory Tonal	Feelings	Auditory Digital

Perfecting The Art Of Telesales Spiced With The Magic Of Neuro-Linguistic Programming

Other patterns to pay attention to:

Visual	Auditory tonal	Feeling	Auditory digital
		Speech *pattern*	
Quickly grouped words	Lots of interruptions and uh, ums, ahs etc.	Slow deliberate phrasing	Long complicated sentences
		Likely *pace*	
Spontaneous/very fast	Decisive/fast	Comfortable/very slow	Systematic/slow
		Processing *pattern*	
Quickly – likely big picture and little detail	Will let you know unconsciously when he understands by changing the subject	Extensive detail	Will not give indication of understanding unless you ask
		Decision *type*	
Spontaneous	Closed/final	Considered	Deliberate
		Time to *act style*	
Can procrastinate	Now!	Then/when	Schedules
		Likely preferred *close*	
Direct	Direct	Assumptive	Detailed summary
		Tone of voice *for close*	
	Slightly fast and excited	Thoughtful, considerate and just slightly above monotone	
		Irritated *by*	
Predictability and lack of imagination	Indecision and slowness	Impatience and pushiness	Surprises or inaccuracy
		Wants telesales *person to be*	
Imaginative and inspired	Decisive and be able to get to the point	Confident, tolerant and friendly	Sensible, precise and accurate

Perfecting The Art Of Telesales *Spiced With The Magic Of Neuro-Linguistic Programming*

The important thing to remember regarding all this, is that you will be 'matching' your prospect from the time he picks up the phone. Match the words he uses, and his tone and speech patterns.

It is important to **actively listening** to how your prospect answers the phone, if he says, "Hello, Bloggs here". **'Match'** and use the **same tone and words** and say, "**Hello**, Mr. Bloggs, its...**here** from..." and then continue.

As opposed to responding with "Good afternoon Mr. Bloggs, it's...from..." which is a mis-match.

The sooner you start to match the quicker you will build rapport.

Examples of closing phrases using sensory based language:

Visual

Closing phrases

If at any time in the call he says, *"I cannot see what you are saying"*

This means you:

"If this looks good to you, we will go ahead and focus on getting the paperwork done"

- Have not created enough of a visual image for him to understand your message and be convinced

"As this is solely your decision, please can you see that I get the purchase order number today, thanks"

- Build more rapport, keep your pace fast

- Choose more visual words and be concise and to the point

- Show him how to access the relevant information or a demonstration on your web site (if possible or applicable)

Product information sent should have pictures, graphs, and diagrams and be showing your product/services only relevant to his need

Service information, with customer references of how it enhanced their company image

Auditory Tonal

Closing phrases

If at any time in the call he says, *"It doesn't sound right to me"*

This means you:

"If this sounds good to you, we will go ahead and discuss how to set up an account"

"If I can just tell you the options, you can choose which you want to order now?"
In asking this question you need to use a 'questioning tone'.

I have written on purpose 'you can choose', rather than 'can you choose'

The reason is that 'you can' in this context, using a certain tone, becomes an embedded command, i.e. implying he will choose

Whereas, if I say 'can you choose' he may say 'no' because it is a closed question.

-   Have not created enough understanding of how it sounds, and he is not yet convinced

-   Build more rapport. Keep your pace even. Maybe use monotone (if this is how he sounds – match his voice and tone)

-   Choose more auditory words to heighten his listening experience

-   Send an audiocassette/CD or have him access a web- based presentation that has sound

Product information sent would be more beneficial to him if it has sound; if not, talk him through it

Whatever you send, ensure that you make follow up calls to this prospect. He needs frequent contact, even when not a lot is said

Service information, with references he can call

Perfecting The Art Of Telesales Spiced With The Magic Of Neuro-Linguistic Programming

Feelings

Closing phrases

If at any time in the call he says, "I cannot grasp your meaning"

This means you:

If this feels good to you, we will go ahead and set up an account by handling the paperwork

"You agree that this feels right for you, great, I feel real good about it too"

"You will feel very contented and proud to own one of these"

- You have not created enough of an emotional charge on the words for him to feel convinced

- Build rapport by keeping your pace slow, warm and sincere

- Choose more emotionally charged words to have him feel good about what you are offering

- Send a sample of the product to feel the texture or finish

Product information sent should show how something feels and looks

Service information with references from satisfied customers with specific comments about how they felt about it

Perfecting The Art Of Telesales *Spiced With The Magic Of Neuro-Linguistic Programming*

Auditory Digital

Closing phrases

If at any time in the call he says, *"It doesn't make sense to me"*

This means you:

"If it makes sense to you, and you know it will work, we will go ahead and process the paperwork"

"Now that we have checked through the specification, I am certain you are in a position to make the decision today.... how many would you like to order?"

- Have not provided sufficient logic, order and reason for him to be convinced

- Build rapport and use your words in a procedural fashion. Keep your pace medium to fast

- Use lots of words, and detail (if this is how he is – match him). Make it easy for him to hear and follow the logical order of what you are proposing

Send specifications, lists. Any contrastive analysis is always of interest. If asked, send quotes, proposals

Product information sent should show the logical order of things. Lots of details about the features but with relevant benefits

Service information with references he can call or with specific detail of how customers benefit

Perfecting The Art Of Telesales Spiced With The Magic Of Neuro-Linguistic Programming

Make up some sensory based closing phrases of your own:

Visual	
Auditory tonal	
Feelings	
Auditory digital	

Perfecting The Art Of Telesales *Spiced With The Magic Of Neuro-Linguistic Programming*

A final reminder:

These Internal Representational Systems (IRs), as the name implies, are a way of describing how you (and everyone else) represents their world. The human brain encodes information from the environment using the five senses. You then use this information internally in a similar fashion. If you like, re-present this information inside yourself to create your experience.

The way you re-present information internally has infinite possibility, you might say it is your very own language. Communication depends on language, be that verbal or non-verbal. Therefore, the greater the similarity of language used between you and your prospect, the stronger the rapport and degree of understanding is likely to be.

These IRs are the way you take in, store and code information and typically in these four modes. Although you can potentially use all of these modes equally well, you will tend to have preferences; preferences created out of the habit of using them.

It is an over-generalization to label yourself (or anyone else) as 'visual' or 'auditory' or 'touchy feely' or 'digital'. However, if you can identify and use the sensory language your prospect is using, it builds rapport, and greater understanding, and you will have a more meaningful conversation. It is as if you are 'talking his language'.

Human behaviour is extremely complex and my only motive here is to have you become aware that there is a lot more going on than perhaps you first thought. The more you become conscious of what is really going on within you, the better you will become at communicating with others. This relates to all contexts of your life, not just telephone selling.

I am outlining a very limited view of how people, in general, describe experience and use words for this purpose. You and I make choices (usually unconsciously) about which words best represent the experience. These words describe the portion of that experience which corresponds to the processes and relationships in that experience.

It was observed by John Grinder and Richard Bandler during their years of research that very little of natural language communication is metaphorical. Most people, they observed, even in casual conversation, describe their experiences quite literally. People who, for example, organize their world primarily with pictures, most often communicate with "I see what you are saying".

I cannot do NLP the justice it deserves in this guidebook, but I trust that I have made you curious about it and that you will investigate this fascinating subject yourself to continue your learning and development.

I know you will begin to listen more closely to yourself and others around you and start to become more conscious at identifying the language triggers and to which sense they belong.

Perfecting The Art Of Telesales Spiced With The Magic Of Neuro-Linguistic Programming

Language trigger exercise:

This is an easy exercise to help you build your skill and awareness[7].

Pick one person a day, perhaps someone you know well, and allow yourself to notice his language triggers. When you think you have identified his preferred IR, ask him directly how is he organizing his experience at that point in time.

If his IR is visual, ask

- Do you make pictures in your head?
- Do you have visual images as you are talking and listening to me?
- Can you see what I am saying?

If his IR is feeling, ask

- Do you feel what you are saying?
- Are you in touch with what I am saying?

If his IR is Auditory, ask

- Do you hear voices in your head?
- Do you hear what I am saying inside your head?
- Are you talking to yourself about what I am saying?
- Do you make lists in your head? (Often makes a physical list)

It is certain you will learn a great deal about yourself and those around you.

Ask any questions that help you understand how people organize their experiences.

Remember humans are infinitely flexible; they may use all of these IRs or only one or two of them.

It is important to say, as a general rule, that the more senses you can engage in telephone conversation the higher the quality of your information and communication.

This exercise will certainly build your active and focused listening skills – ready for more successful telephone selling.

---

[7] "The Structure of Magic II", John Grinder and Richard Bandler, Science and Behaviour Books Inc. Used with kind permission.

Perfecting The Art Of Telesales *Spiced With The Magic Of Neuro-Linguistic Programming*

Telesales maps

Richard Bandler and John Grinder developed a model of how we communicate to others and ourselves. Their model explains how we process the information that comes to us from the outside. The presupposition ('convenient belief') is that " The map is not the territory" and so the internal representations that we make about an outside event are not necessarily the event itself - only our version of it.

Typically, what happens is:

- we run an event through our internal processing

- we make an internal representation (IR) of that event

- the IR of the event combines with our body via our nervous system and creates an emotional state – happy, motivated, excited, etc.

- this IR includes our internal pictures, sounds and self-talk, and our feelings (for example, whether we feel motivated, challenged, pleased, excited, confident and so on)

The emotional state is the result of an external event passing through our senses; the process of filtering creates an internal representation made up of pictures, sounds, feelings and self-talk.

On the next few pages are two examples of the maps of two successful telesales people:

- Jacquie Christoforou, whose IRs are primarily pictures/feelings

- Brenda Spiller whose IRs are primarily auditory tonal/digital

The examples highlight how both of us unconsciously follow and use the basic structure of the telesales call by utilizing our preferred IRs. It also shows how 'behaviour' results from all this processing at different levels.

These different levels are aspects of ourselves that we would not ordinarily recognize or pay attention to because we are not conscious of them. They are known in NLP as Neurological Levels, developed by Robert Dilts from a model originated by anthropologist Gregory Bateson.

To accelerate your learning, through NLP and Robert Dilt's wonderful work you will come to realize that while changing something on an upper level will **always** make a difference at a lower level, the reverse is not necessarily true; i.e. changing something at a lower level can, but does not necessarily, affect the upper level.

For example, if you change what you **believe**, you will certainly **change what you do.** However, if you change your **environment it does not necessarily change your behaviour,** because a change in behaviour will not last unless there is a higher value or belief to support it. The following are the levels we used to map our unconscious and unique telesales structures

Level	In life	In telephone selling
Spirituality	Why are we here, what is our purpose?	To help you create meaningful and positive change (results) for your higher good in a way that is quick, simple, easy and lasting
Identity	Our sense of self	Who are we when we are telephone selling and what is our purpose?
Beliefs and values	What we permit ourselves to do or not, and what is important to us	What do we believe about ourselves when we are telephone selling, what is important and why?
Capability	Our competencies	What skills do we have and exhibit as a telesales person?
Behaviour	Actions we carry out regardless of competence	What we do when acting as a telesales person?
Environment	Our surroundings – who and what we react to	Where and when do we act as a telesales person?

Interestingly, we discovered even that without knowledge of NLP (I only did my formal training after three decades in telesales.) that we changed from being unconscious incompetents to conscious unconscious competents, through consistently practising telephone selling over the years. Unconsciously we had fine-tuned our skills to the extent that we became very successful, knew what worked and repeated those patterns.

We learned too, how to make subtle changes by paying attention and noticing what happened, doing something different and noticing the change that made the difference. For us, this has been almost a working lifetime's process, and in hindsight unnecessarily slow. For you, we trust you will learn fast by using the information in this guidebook and through NLP.

In these examples we have also included the motivation and working traits, convincers and decision factors that we use.

Perfecting The Art Of Telesales *Spiced With The Magic Of Neuro-Linguistic Programming*

Telesales maps

The author's goal for this map:	To provide you an example of the unconscious patterns used by a person who has **phenomenal success** telephone selling.

This example is the map of Jacquie Christoforou's telesales world. Jacquie has made telephone selling a career and almost an art form. She has been doing it consistently for more than 25 years. We have uncovered some of her unconscious patterns of behaviour that determine her continuing success and outstanding performance.

Jacquie, has done telephone selling in advertising (telephone directories), recruitment, training and has worked for the last 15 years in her own telemarketing business working with her customers in the security, IT, manufacturing and training industries.

Her initial attraction to telephone selling as a career was driven by a need for change and to succeed, and although she never really wanted to be in management, she managed a telesales team for a number of years, and became a highly sought after telesales trainer.

Jacquie's telesales goals:	For Jacquie, success is related specifically to stability - always moving towards maintaining this, and away from giving anyone else the opportunity to control her destiny. She sets her own targets and an expectation then achieves them. Even though past employers and current customers set targets, it is without doubt that Jacquie's own will be far more challenging.

When she worked within a team – she needed to be the best, and liked beating the others, but more important was setting and achieving own targets.

Now as a self-employed telesales person her goal is still the achievement of her defined targets, not her customer's. The intention to make money for both, and of course to keep her customers happy, and has ensured contracts over a long-term period for her ongoing security.

Her number one rule:	Always dress for business. Jacquie was in a smart business suit when I arrived to do the interview. The office was organized and ready for work.
Her valuable piece of advice to you:	"If you are not prepared **to achieve** don't do this job. You cannot play around at this, do it wholeheartedly, or not at all"

Jacquie's 'map of her telesales world':

Creating her prospecting list

First of all a list of suspects is obtained or created. (To remind you, these are companies you may want to do business with, that you want to qualify into prospects. Your list can be the companies in a given industry sector or territory.)

Jacquie never calls a list systematically – but she will call **every** company on the list at some point.

'Creaming process' – Jacquie's term for picking the juiciest companies on the list – her intention – to call them first.

The companies are 'looked' at in order to 'see and feel' (location of feeling mid chest, straight line down to top of stomach area – pleasant excited feeling) how 'big' they are. She 'creates a panoramic image' of the company in 'black and white', 'focused', the building is always 'white', has 'steps leading up to the doorway', and she expands this image from the 'doorway with pillars' into a full blown factory or office complex, even creates what may be going on inside the company once she is conversation with her prospect.

- Segmentation of the list - the 'big' ones on the list are the key to prioritizing the prospects – she looks for - Ltd, Europe, and Plc in the company names, and of course the well-known companies

- Addresses e.g. 9 Fairly Close wouldn't 'hit has hard' as Stanton House, Stanton Place particularly if the company was also called Stanton. She would pick Stanton as this 'looks and sounds' (telling herself that it is) bigger in her mind. A business that is located on a business park or industrial estate might indicate it is large.

- Building numbers play an importance in selection – 200 – 204, The High Street would be higher on the list than 3 Heather Road – makes it 'feel' larger - another big clue

- Companies with many departments - qualify as big

- Company names – e.g. in security Joseph and Son may 'feel smaller' (possibly only two people) whereas in manufacturing Hargreaves Atkins Brewery (indicates lots of people) – in this situation the 'pictures become a little fuzzy and the feeling flattens' out but the feeling remains in the same location

- Telephone numbers – companies with 2000, 3000, 2151 likely larger organizations

- Size of company will also determine whom you call first – numbers of people employed and/or turnover. 400 employees with £70 million call them first, 40 employees with £10 million would also qualify for a call whereas 40 employees with £1 million would feature lower down on the list, but would be called at some point

- Number of branches the company has, is an indication they may be 'big'

- Contacts – named contacts – knows she has to check them always – if list has been recently validated prior to telephone selling she may use the contact names as a quick means of entry, but will still check them

- Departments and titles - if the list has people with department or function listed, this is important if wanting to find a specific title – those listed with the title will be called first – if there is a contact name this will be validated

Summary:

1. If the company listed meets Jacquie's internal criteria i.e. 'white building and excited feeling, and the size of the company (numbers of people and job title/function is stated etc) – she gets a more intense excited state, and is 'certain' this is the one to call.

2. Marks all those companies within these categories – calls them first.

3. All the rest of the companies are called, but the priority calls are those who meet her internal 'look and feel' barometer. Nothing is ever missed.

**Unusual
contacts**

There are also 'odd occurrences' where the company name on the list appears to be 'calling to her', like a connection. These are companies she would not list as priorities but she is 'drawn to make contact' and they turn out to be right

(Having had this experience myself on a number of occasions it is a totally 'intuitive' reaction to the name and address on the page. The 'pull is so strong' it has to be called – it's a 'knowing' – absolute trust in following the drive to make the call. It is almost like receiving an 'incoming call from this prospect without the use of the telephone' – I think we will call this telepathy as the best description – but let me not stray too far from the plot.)

The contrast inside Jacquie for this type of call is – 'no image' – a 'feeling surrounds her at chest and shoulders' – a 'feeling/sense outside' of herself – 'no sounds' , however on making the call she talks to herself "this is good after all" all mundane chatter "I didn't know about this one, I just needed to call it" . In the call she will also 'hear' something that confirms it's a good one i.e. 'big' could be what sounds like large machinery or movement of vehicles, the hub hub of people talking, anything that indicates there is something going on.

I also noticed at this point a dramatic shift in Jacquie's facial expression:

- On the calls where she is 'connected by this calling to her', her face is smooth, happy expression, no lines in her forehead. In these calls she also has to concentrate on not showing 'too much excitement' in her voice – just thinking to herself "this is a goody"

- Whereas those companies who are likely small and/or not so good, her face is creased as if in mild pain, serious expression and lines on her forehead

The Art Of Telephone Selling *Spiced With The Magic Of Neuro-Linguistic Programming*

189

Environment
Where and when does she act as a telesales person?

Jacquie needs a secluded, quiet, enclosed space, and preferably no other people around. It must be bright, she must be able to see clearly, be comfortable, have a clear desk, and the shelf space tidy i.e. no clutter around.

- All product/service information and terms of business on the right of the desk. The list of questions to be asked is always directly in front of her

- Telephone to the left. Calls more relaxed if using a headset rather than a handset

- All equipment working properly is important to the success of her day. Her customers (as in her work life now) must provide her with all necessary information in time for her days work. She can be put off by a customer's inefficiency to provide necessary information that supports her telephone selling; this affects her getting on with her starting on time. It breaks her concentration, and adds 'pressure in her head, like bolts at the back of the neck'. When this happens it takes her longer to get into the days calling – in turn she ends up working longer hours – but still completes her committed 6 hours per day

(Many years ago Jacquie was part of my telesales team, I can confirm that in a room of 25+ telesales people, she still created this environment for herself, even within a large open plan office. Her desk was clear, except she created a secluded space by surrounding herself with boxes containing her prospect customer cards (no PCs in those days), her side bin (desk with lid) was always raised open to giver her the appearance of being in a secluded place, she effectively shut out the rest of the team all day, and did not speak with them.)

She gets into a 'positive working space' – every calling day.

Behaviour

What does she do when she is acting as a telesales person?

Before entering her office she will start her day thinking about what she wants to achieve and what she is to do. This thinking drives up the energy - moving from stomach area towards her chest - a positive excited feeling.

Also prior to entering her office to work, she makes a **commitment to herself outside the door** about what she wants **to achieve**. Then walks through the door - **committed, in a great mood, and looking forward to the day.**

She sets aside 6 hours for dedicated calling activity. On some occasions her calling activity will be adjusted to suit the workload, for example, with some industries who start earlier in the day e.g. manufacturing - she will make calls from 8 a.m. onwards. The earlier start often means she makes 4 good presentations in an hour, whereas if she calls after 9 a.m. it may take her 3 hours and many more calls to achieve the same result.

Flexibility is important.

When things are not working well – she checks product information, or her approach with her customer (this will be the customer she is telephone selling on behalf of) - asks for feedback – checks that she is not the problem. Must act so in order not to become complacent. When she confirms she is not the problem – telephone selling resumes.

External checks like this only happen once in a while, but are important to the consistency with which her success is achieved.

Capabilities
What skills does she have and exhibit as a telesales person?

'Feels excited', especially if it is a brand new list. 'Very hyped up - feeling in mid chest'.

Initial/cold calls

- **Dials out number – no contact:**

  - If cannot reach anyone – accepts it as par for the course – excitement remains – calling continues
  - Works systematically down her 'creamed list'
  - If a large number of calls have been attempted, and no one is available, her feeling changes to 'tenseness and stress' but energy has changed to help her carry on – striving and more determined than ever – eventually reaches a prospect and its all worthwhile – commonly at times like this, it is the last call of the day that will provide a stunning result, even may be one of the one's she is drawn too, but she keeps her goal in mind – selling

- **Dial out number and makes a contact:**

  - States who she is
  - Why she is calling
  - Checks he is the correct person
  - Questioning commences

During questioning she is seeking information about the prospect's environment, situation and needs, and as he answers those questions then her internal 'pictures and feelings' start to build. She 'pictures':

- The prospect– environment he is in – these pictures are 'moving' from the white building to becoming a fuller image of the business - its departments, people moving about, whole factories, machinery moving etc.

- She has a heightened awareness of the prospect's reactions, and importantly **how she will react to him.** Noticing what is going on in the conversation, e.g. pitch, pace and his tone of voice. When his voice tone changes, she thinks "what did I say that changed his tone – if the voice level has gone down – she re-questions to bring it back up. Better questioning changes the tonality – remembering it is key to have the prospect feel good about the conversation

- All the time she is trying to get inside his brain, this would 'look like a feeling of comfort'. She wants him to know that she is on the phone not to just come out with a sale, but to have him realize, that if he does not have a need, she won't force him to do something against his wishes

- She re-checks what is important to him in order to make sure she using his, and her own time effectively

Questioning is the key to build up her knowledge of his situation, to give him the best for his business, and show how her knowledge of what she is selling is the solution to his need.

Establishment of a need:

- **If he has no need**

- Concentrates on making him feel good about the call and herself, because he may have a need another time – so gains permission to call back (even if in a years time) – which she will do, and he will always remember her

- Her evidence is the prospect's voice which is at a high pleasurable level, he may say "its been good to talk to you, thanks for calling". Relief is heard in his voice, that she has accepted that he has no need - right now

- Jacquie is grateful that he came to the phone to say he has no needs, it could save her additional calls trying to contact him needlessly if he is just never available

- She leaves the call still in a happy frame of mind it was a good call even if he didn't have needs

- Calling continues

- **Has a need**

  - Wants to finish the call with him feeling as excited as she is, and knowing he has actions to follow upon as a result – that she will be calling back to progress the sale

  - Always leaves him with an action or expectation e.g. he has to speak with someone else – she will check when he will do it – and arrange her call back date accordingly

  - If he wants information – she checks how long he may need to go through it, and gets agreement to a call back date

  - If she knows it's a 'goer' i.e. a sale will result - she is very excited – feeling in chest area becomes more expansive and intense

  - At end of call – makes comprehensive notes on prospect record – and notes whether a 'hot' prospect i.e. the one, which she deems, are goers' or certainly in 'buy mode'

  - Diarises a call back (even a year ahead if needs be) sends any information on email/post immediately

  - Everything to do with this call is completed before next call

  - Makes next call

A note on closing

Providing the prospect has some experience of the product/service it is possible to close the sale and get the business on an initial or cold call. However, for most telesales people it will invariably take more than one call.

Follow up calls

Jacquie's initial patterns for commencing follow up calls is the same as initial/cold calls, however on entering the office and looking at the diary of call backs, Jacquie's 'feelings' are 'excited' and/or increased to 'very excited' or 'immensely excited' dependent upon the number of calls and quality.

There may be some that do not excite, but positive thinking and hard work helps to create miracles, the point is **she never gives up.**

Follow up calling is never out of her mind, she thinks about them maybe a week before the activity.

- **Few callbacks:**

  - Looks at each one – reads notes – makes decision which to call first – calls them all. Goes back to cold calling when finished call backs

- **High number of callbacks:**

  - Those noted as 'hot' would be called first – always does good calls first, sets up the day with success

  - Looks at individual calls and makes the call – feels excitement (in same location) and based upon on what is in her notes, will assess likely outcome – remembers pictures from previous call – 'visualizes the prospect's action, and its positive outcomes' e.g. if he was having a meeting with others, she pictures the meeting and its positive outcome i.e. a decision in her favour

  - Makes the call
    - Re-introduces self
    - Recap previous conversation
    - Reminds him of things they said and agreed to – what he agreed to do – prospect usually laughs – this raises his energy
    - Most important to remind why he had asked for information or had a meeting to discuss it
    - Asks about the outcome of his actions
    - Decide the next steps as he sees it – as he explains, she visualizes what he says about how the product/service fits into his plans

- If she cannot visualize how or at what point the product/service fits in – she asks him how he sees it fitting in – his description must 'intensify her picture', and she must see that last piece of the jigsaw fits before closing

- Jacquie also talks to herself at this point asking, "am I there yet, is what he is saying realistic and true"

- Has to establish a clear picture, and if a piece is missing – makes another call back – she would rather make another call than have any doubts

- Any doubts – she re-validates that he is definitely interested, and he agrees for her to call back again. Her feeling is exciting but lower key

- When picture is absolutely clear of benefits to both sides – she closes – asks for order. Clarifies final administration points, and any processes to be followed

- After the call Jacquie is very excited and will feel she has achieved something for both herself and her prospect

- Onto next call

Success always building on success

2nd Follow up call   Pattern as described previously for follow up calls

- Introduction
- Recap
- Remind
- What he agreed to do – waiting for the last piece of the jigsaw
- Close

- **No sale yet but possible for future**

  - Do process again – give instructions – do whatever needs to be done – keeps following up – setting timescales in agreement with prospect

  - **Never lets go** call backs are determined by situation e.g. – redundancies – bow out for a time – call back in a year. Takeovers, mergers, re organizations, change of personnel – keeps calling – manages timescales of call in relation to company's situation

- **If no go i.e. a complete waste of time** – this is usually established on the first call (which may take 20 minutes to find out) Jacquie is very thorough on the first call

  - Then leave alone until another time – maybe another year

- **No sale - chosen another supplier**

  - Same pattern as follow up calls

  - When told no sale – feeling moves to disappointment and felt in the same location

  - Jacquie questions why he chose another company - the timescales on the decision to reconfirm he made the right decision – if pilot or trial of chosen company's product/service – call again and see how it went – this becomes the reason for the call – checking prospect is happy with expected outcome on his decision – if not as he expected, he may well be convinced to use the product/services Jacquie is selling instead

  - If prospect happy with his decision – agree to call back in a year – calls back in a year to check the product/service he bought is still meeting expectation – if not check what he is going to do about it – if going to change – ask when – keep in contact again – telephone selling starts over

  - If she 'feels' he really and absolutely means 'no' and she cannot persuade him around – she leaves it and closes the call – keeps company on a list for a future and/or may find another contact in the organization

Calls to existing customers

A call to an existing customer is subjected to the same rigorous internal criteria – Jacquie always remembers that she is **selling!**

- When she finds a need – closes immediately

- Cross selling – she looks for options to cross sell (sell different products/services to same customer – looks for new prospects for products/services)

  - If a new contact in same company

  - Recalls the company – does not asked to be transferred, unless it is offered

- Always uses existing contact as a way in – i.e. this becomes the reason for the call

- Uses exactly the same process, and adds to her existing pictures, this new prospect, his department and situation as he describes it, and answers her questions

Cancellation of her services

Jacquie's skill at 'relationship building' means that customer loyalty and trust is very strong. When customers move away from using Jacquie's services it would be for a very valid reason, and unlikely because he is going to use another supplier, and when she is told that the contract is going to be terminated, she immediately asks herself:

- What do I need to do?

- Thinks replace, replace, replace

- Thinks of others who could be the replacement
  In her current business all of her existing clients either know her or have been recommended. Some have never met her but have been so highly recommended they have been happy to discuss things over the telephone and then commence using her services, however she still creates a list of potential companies and keeps one ready just in case

- If necessary she would cold call and keep calling until she replaced her contract (this is how she originally built up her business)

Beliefs and values

What does she believe about herself when she is telephone selling and what is important to her and why?

What is important to Jacquie is being in control of herself – knowing the power of how much control people may have over her.

Every day is a fight, a challenge for survival, and her motivation towards her goal is that her success will give her the things she wants to be comfortable, and in maintaining her security.

Motivation is driven by a need to be the best because this gives control on how people react to her – when working within a team providing she was very successful – people (management) left her alone. (In my team she was the best, she knew it, she knew I knew it, and I left her alone – her performance was outstanding and still is.)

Success brings freedom. Highly competitive too - always wants to beat others. Always feels confident that she will do well.

Now working for herself, her motivation is much the same, her drive to maintain her freedom to utilize her time to her advantage, and achieve her dreams and maintain her stability.

Believes and knows she is good at telesales. No doubt in her mind. She wants to achieve, and is happy because telesales is a challenge.

Believes she is capable of delivery of whatever is set for her, and as long as she has a 'skimpy' understanding of the product or service, (and she must have this knowledge, if not it will hold her back – is pedantic for the knowledge of the product/service but in a simple way i.e. it must be easy to explain.) Is then able to use her business skills to segment product/service knowledge from sales skills and industry knowledge – gets a feel and asks relevant questions. She believes you must know all about the company you work for, not just own department.

Very strong belief that every sale is 'ongoing' nothing is ever a 'one off'. The prospect must have a real need; know what he wants, and what you have to offer to solve it. Won't push a sale that doesn't exist.

The Art Of Telephone Selling *Spiced With The Magic Of Neuro-Linguistic Programming*

Identity

Who is she when
telephone selling

- Highly self motivated
- Happy
- Territorial
- Aggressive
- Stubborn
- Very channeled – focused way of thinking
- Very positive
- Very determined
- Never gives up
- Excellent time keeper
- Disciplined
- Persistent
- Organized

When making calls – is joined with the prospect – the conversation – her senses are all immersed in the call.

'Whole self' in the call, cannot judge how prospect is feeling unless connected.

Can tell when a prospect is:

- Doing something else
- Not finding what she says appealing
- Or is excited by what she says

Must operate as a whole in the call

No distractions – she becomes incensed if there is an unnecessary interruption to the call.

In my interview with Jacquie, many of her unconscious patterns were a surprise to her, but consistent throughout the testing of each aspect of her telesales calling structure.

For the purpose of interest in respect of 'adding the spice of NLP' her internal representations (IRs) are predominately visual and feeling, often totally connected i.e. if she had a picture there was a feeling and vice versa, some auditory tonal – sounds, and occasional self-talk. For Jacquie these particular preferences work for her, and over the years she has no doubt unconsciously tested, refined and aligned them to her total understanding and use of the telesales call structure.

Jacquie in a telesales context exhibits the following traits:

Motivation traits:

- Proactive
- Towards with a little away from
- Internal and external - primarily internal
- Procedures – which she has developed for herself over the years (which means she possibly started with options – and now her tried and tested methods work best)
- Sameness with exception

Her convincers about her prospects are:

- See - Do - Hear

Working traits

- Specific – she works with lots of details and checks detail for the purpose of telephone selling. This is not to say she doesn't see the bigger picture, but the refinement and success of the sale requires detail

Her decision factors for closing on her prospects

- Consistent – she re checks and re checks information

- Period of time – used only as dictated by the prospects buying process

- Automatic – when an existing customer, and real need and opportunity presents itself

The Art Of Telephone Selling Spiced With The Magic Of Neuro-Linguistic Programming

The author
My goals for
this map:

To provide you with a contrasting example of the unconscious patterns for successful telephone selling.

(The examples demonstrate the uniqueness of two people, who having developed and refined their styles and methods of telephone selling are both successful)

Other notes:

I do telephone selling intermittently these days but it still plays a vital role in the success of my consultancy and training business.

The initial attraction to telephone selling as a career was driven by a need for change from a boring public sector job; and a thought that I was going to help save people's lives (I was going into safety training) not realizing I was going to be telephone selling, and ultimately earning a lot more money.

(I must add at this point, at first I absolutely detested telephone selling and after 3 weeks I was never going to do it again, and here I am some 30 years later – the moral of my tale – a change of mind or heart can bring much good fortune!)

Telesales has brought me a fortune in money, good health, much happiness and truly wonderful friends.

My telesales
goals:

In my early years to manage my single parent status, which ensured stability for my daughter, and that I had enough money to pay my bills, and do well in the world.

Now - to maintain my lifestyle business – that maintains my expensive and interesting lifestyle – to provide security for my two grandchildren – to share my wealth and have good times with my friends.

My number
one rule:

Dream, think, believe, and act successfully.

My valuable
piece of
advice to you:

"Follow rule one and you will be successful, in whatever that means for you."

The Art Of Telephone Selling Spiced With The Magic Of Neuro-Linguistic Programming

My 'map of my telesales world':

Creating my prospecting list

- 'Talk to myself' (sometimes out loud) about what I am going to do - have an even tone of voice (my voice) - sound very convincing as if I know what I am doing – believe myself - it all sounds very logical

- Create an 'ideal customer profile' i.e. those I would like to do business with – defined by industry sector, physical location, size of company – number of branches, employees and turnover, and likely issues that can be addressed by using my services. Just 'know' prospects have people with behavioural challenges – an ability to 'sense' the problems – also draw from knowledge gained from management and other training I have had

- Usually create a list of suspects from a bought and partially validated list

- Segment the list by the well-known companies first and ask myself "Are they growing, declining, or stable organizations". I pick the ones in 'growth mode' and call them first. (Growing companies are generally sales driven and so are easier to sell to – i.e. the concept that what you are offering will help them grow faster – generate more revenue – more profit.) I then call those on the 'declining' list – although these companies are generally cost driven, so tend to be cost conscious, but anything that helps them save money or make better use of it will interest them – so I target them. Stable companies need to move into growth or decline to attract me to call them

- Address - is not important – but location is i.e. the areas I am prepared to travel to, and from. For example, London does not fall into my location criteria, as a consequence I never prospect into London, however, occasionally customers come to me by default, but I never actively seek them out

- Companies need specific departments - sales, customer services and technical support groups

- Company names – play no part in my selection other than to highlight those to avoid i.e. companies who are not my ideal customers - mostly well known corporations, I would not for example prospect to Barclays Bank, Marks & Spencer, Microsoft, or any Government departments. (In a lifestyle buisness one can make these decisions)

- Size of company in terms of numbers of employees will always determine whom I call first – based on my ideal customer profile

- Contacts – named contacts – use them if they are relevant - re validate them - mostly find my own contacts based on roles and responsibilities that are likely to be interested in my types of services

- Departments and titles - this is important if wanting to find a specific title – those listed with the title will be called first – if there is a contact name this will be validated

Summary:

- If the company listed meets my 'ideal customer profile', it is a suspect. I have no image or feelings about them at all

- I mark all these companies within these categories – call them first

- All the rest of the companies in the same industry sector would be called, but the priority calls are those who meet my specific criteria

- If I were telephone selling all day every day I would also work industry by industry

Unusual contacts

There are also 'odd occurrences' where the company name on the list needs to be called.

I just 'know' I have to call it, almost as if I hear someone say, "this is the one" or "call me, call me". I trust my intuition and call – invariably it is the right decision.

I can remember a specific incident when this occurred. Mid 1980s, working for a software company at the time I was looking through job advertisements for suspects, when I came across a company called then 'Financial Insurance Group' - the name FIG called out to me.

I called four times, and was 'fobbed off' by the receptionist but I left a message each time, on my fourth call, (she was fed up with me calling), and said "The man has just arrived from the USA, and is new to the company, he won't want to talk to you now".

My response was "If he is new, then he needs some friends, and needs to know about suppliers like us, why don't you ask him if he wants to talk to me, I'll wait". She did, and he came to the phone and said, "I have your four messages I just wanted to see how tenacious you were, and I do have a requirement".

He told me right off the bat, that he had a need. The only thing I had to do was take down the information he gave me, and sort out the details of our response.

I am making it sound simplistic, but the point is, we were not in a competitive situation, he never called anyone else, we provided what he wanted, when he wanted it, and over a 2 year period that initial 'call me' contact netted the company £250,000+ worth of business.

Environment

Where and when do I act as a telesales person?

These days I only act as a telesales person intermittently between delivery of training courses and keeping in contact with existing customers. However, I have answered these questions 'as if' I was doing the job fulltime i.e. as I used too.

I have a preference for being on my own, but can work with others around me, and mentally shut them out, unless they are talking in such low tones, where I can only audibly hear the drone of their voices, but not specifically what is being said – this I find irritating. The only real distraction would be music - this interferes with my concentration.

- All product/service information and terms of business would need to 'sound logical' to me. I couldn't sell something that didn't 'make sense'. I hold a conversation with the prospect in my head - testing out the questions and possible responses before making the call (needless to say he gives me all the right answers!). Note down the questions I had exercised in my mental discussion – ask these ones initially - will add questions that go with the logic and flow of the conversation

- The telephone can be anywhere on the desk - always use a headset - hearing piece must be on my left ear – for actively listening - tuning in my intuition – all works better using this ear

- The atmosphere and energy around my head is 'hot'

Behaviour

What do I do when I am acting as a telesales person?

- I am always in a positive frame of mind. I get up everyday and decide I am having another great day today

- I tell myself I will talk with some interesting prospects, and they will be interested, and buy my services

- 6-7 hours for dedicated calling activity - adjust the calling activity to suit the workload - call very early and very late in the day to avoid the 'gatekeepers' and to maximize on when senior people are likely sitting at their desks - call during lunchtime

- When things are not working well - move to next call quickly - keep going until I find someone who is positive and willing to speak - never expend energy on someone who doesn't sound interested - make arrangements to call at another time, maybe later that same day – when they are not interested apart from what they say to me – the energy around my head goes from 'hot to cool' – I pick up the 'coolness' as soon as they answer. If it is sort of 'warmish' I might keep the conversation going until there is a definite increase/decrease in the temperature

The Art Of Telephone Selling *Spiced With The Magic Of Neuro-Linguistic Programming*

Capabilities

What skills do I have and exhibit as a telesales person?

Initial/cold calls

Dials out number – no contact:

- If cannot reach anyone – accept it as par for the course – positive state of mind remains – calling continues
- Works systematically down the list, or systematically backwards, as I often think that those companies at the end of the alphabet probably get fewer calls than those at the beginning
- If completes list, and no one is available I start over, recalling some of the ones I had tried earlier
- I would have at least 60/70 suspects ready to call

• Dial out number and makes a contact:

- State who I am
- Why I am calling
- Check authority of the person I am calling in relation to my service
- Questioning commences

- During questioning I seek information about the prospect's environment, situation and needs, and as he answers those questions I make copious notes of what he tells me

- I write notes on the left of the page of things he has 'no interest' in

- 'Things of interest' I write on the right side of the page

- I underline points to be re-checked or validated; and any contradictory statements he makes

- I make notes of words and phrases he uses, for example, if he says words like:

  - "We…" I later check to find out who the 'we' is he is referring to
  - "A decision was made in the past about…" I ask how and who arrived at the decision and what would happen if they had made a different decision
  - "We did xyz before, and it didn't work" I ask what specifically did you do, when, what was the expectation, what was the actual result, what would you do differently given an opportunity

The Art Of Telephone Selling Spiced With The Magic Of Neuro-Linguistic Programming

- I listen to the tonality of his voice for:

    - Disbelief, excitement, fear, anxiety, vagueness
    - When he is not quite telling me all the facts or the truth
    - Shadows behind his words, hesitancy, pregnant pauses i.e. silence in the wrong place
    - Inability to answer a question – he nervously clears his throat
    - Speed of speech increasing or slowing
    - When he is distracted by someone or something else

- I listen for

    - Atmospherics in and around him – and note the changes in temperature and energy around me
    - Hub hub in the background possible people talking or entering his office
    - Other phones ringing he may need to answer, and I check if he wants to answer it
    - I can sense 'heaviness' in the call or conversely 'lightness' by his willingness to talk or laugh or maybe just keep to the point, and be business like

- I have a highly attuned sense of the whole conversation as if I am outside myself 'listening in' on two people talking. I spend a lot of time in silence I actively listen. My note taking is rapid – brain writing – taking down the words he says, without the need at this moment to make sense of what he said

- I need to gain a broad understanding of the organization - to be able to have my service and his need 'click into place in my mind' - then summarize back to him what he told me in a logical sequence - then tell him how my services supports his requirements - perhaps give him specific examples of my work or that of my associates i.e. the testimonials that have a direct match to his need

- Having summarized – re-validate the points I need to - gain his agreement this is what he has told me - gain agreement about what needs to happen next

- In note taking, if he mentions any social aspects of his life – like going on holiday this coming week – I note it – to wish him 'happy holidays' at the end of the conversation

Questioning is the key to build up my knowledge of his situation, to give him the right solution, and tell him how I will help – demonstrate my desire to help – build his desire to buy

Establishment of a need:

- **If he has no need**

  - I tell him, he doesn't appear to have one that I can satisfy at this present time. He agrees. I thank him for his time and confirm we will speak again in a time frame he sets. I will also ask if he knows of anyone else in his organization that may benefit from the service

  - If there is another possible contact I will ask him to transfer me through, and I will start the process over

  - If not, I thank him again, and wish him well and confirm I will contact him again in 6-months/a year's time

  - I diarise the call back

  - I update the contact record

  - Calling continues

- **Has a need**

  - Want to finish the call with him in a positive and decisive state of mind

  - If he is the decision maker and he absolutely agrees he needs my training service, I get out my diary and ask him to fix provisional dates for the courses, and he can check these with the participants

  - If he is the influencer and needs to check with his boss, or another manager whose team may also be attending training I give him these actions to follow upon – offer provisional dates to check – inform or tell him that I will be calling back to progress the sale. Alternatively, sometimes I suggest I will speak to the other manager if I think this will speed up the sale – but I need his agreement to do this

- Always leaves him with an action - and arrange call back date accordingly

- If he wants course information – I check his training objectives and emphasize on topics i.e. what he wants – and ask him to reconfirm what he intends to do with it (so I do not waste time writing it up and he does nothing with it) - gain agreement to a call back date – usually check most convenient time of day too

- If I know it's a 'goer' i.e. a sale will result – I get a 'buzzing of energy' around and inside the top my head – not hot or cool nor warm – more a sound

- At end of call – I make comprehensive notes on contact record – make a list of any questions or points to ask/tell on next call – note provisional dates – his actions – call back date

- Diarises a call back, send any information on email/post immediately

- Everything to do with this call is completed before next call

- Make next call

A reminder on closing   Providing the prospect has some experience of the product/service it is possible to close the sale and get the business on an initial or cold call. However, for most telesales people it will invariably more than one call.

Follow up calls

I check my diary for follow up calls, they are listed with contact name and phone number, I know which ones I can close - call those first.

- **Callbacks**:

  - I read notes – check list of questions/points to ask/tell, if any - rehearse in my head the conversation I am about to have – add any additional questions or points to my list

  - Make the call

    - Re-introduce self
    - Recap previous conversation
    - Remind him of things we agreed
    - Asks for the decision reached:

  - If 'yes' is going ahead, gain agreement of next steps, and inform or tell him that I will write and confirm the arrangements

  - If his company has a purchase order system he can organize this, and I will call for the number, unless he can get it now. (I do not need the purchase order number but some companies insist. I always write and confirm the booking and resend my terms of business)

  - If 'not sure', or 'now has other queries', ask what the specific query is. If he has a specific objection - isolate - question it - get commitment that if I answer it he will buy – answer it – close

  - If 'others' are now involved (sometimes training requirements stretch across several different but linked departments) - get his agreement to speak with each one directly (this would always be my preference) and/or give him the questions to go ask them - agree another call back to get the decision

  - Also check what he thinks 'the others' views will be - if he thinks its likely a negative response - ask him why he is bothering to see it through - if his answer is convincing enough to me, he will likely convince them. If it isn't - I tell him I don't think he is truly convinced, and I may withdraw from this opportunity - sometimes my withdrawal fires him up (sometimes it doesn't) - he asks me to wait for a decision

- This withdrawal more often has the desired effect i.e. that he is the one applying the pressure on his colleagues, and not me, i.e. he is the one who is trying to sell the service. He is then left with the job of convincing his colleagues to buy

- If he thinks the outcome will be positive - he is totally convinced - and I am convinced that he is - then I let him spend his time on it - wait for his decision – obtain a call back date - call then

- If I cannot get him to be specific - ask him outright if he is 'not interested' - I give him permission to say 'no' to me - he usually laughs - sounds relieved – thanks me for being so understanding – usually offers a next time opportunity – which he may follow through on and call me – I will certainly remind him next time I call

- I thank him for his interest in the services – reconfirm that I will be of service some day – move swiftly on to another prospect - keep this company on my list - call again in 6 months to see what has changed or is now required

- Go back to cold calling when I have finished call backs

2ⁿᵈ Follow up call

If my prospect has been sent on 'a mission' to answer my questions of the 'others' and get their commitment

- Introduction
- Recap
- Remind
- Ask him what he found out
- What decision has now been reached
- Deal with the booking if 'yes'
- Thank him for his efforts if 'no'. I would not make any attempt to answer any objections as there are too many people in the process, and I would need to deal with each one. So I have to make a judgment about the value of my time vs. the value of this particular opportunity - is it worth my while - Had he agreed with me earlier, that I speak with each of them, I would not be in this position. how attractive is it to me to continue. If I think it is, I do – if not I bring it to a close

In most circumstances, with my particular services, when a prospect goes off to seek agreement of others, he usually does this because the decision is going to be affirmative.

He would not generally waste his own time if he didn't think he could persuade them. He has now put his own reputation at stake with me and his colleagues, as to whether he gets what he wants, in this case to get training booked and organized. He will work hard at proving himself, and I will get the business.

- **No sale yet but possible for future**

  - I keep following up – setting timescales in agreement with prospect

  - Call backs are determined by situation e.g. – redundancies – sometime attempt to convince him that with less people training is more important - but more often leave for another time – call back in a year or if it becomes apparent that things are getting better call sooner – may see information in the press – share price increasing – hiring more people etc.

  - Takeovers, mergers, re organizations, change of personnel – keep in touch and find out the facts about what is going on and keep comprehensive notes – get agreement on call backs in relation to company's situation - when he becomes receptive – start selling again

The Art Of Telephone Selling Spiced With The Magic Of Neuro-Linguistic Programming

- **If no go i.e. a complete waste of time** – this is usually established on the first call – by energy and temperature!

  - I never waste time trying to convince prospects to buy if they are 'lukewarm' (the atmosphere is cool, no energy coming forth i.e. as if he is not there); there are too many prospects that are already convinced of the value of training. I will go back to those with limited interest later, or if I ever run out of other prospects – which I never have

  - Then leave alone until another time – maybe another year

  - I also use the reverse psychology approach, i.e. I always remind him in a nice way, that I as the supplier have a choice too, and I don't have to work for him, and I never, that is never, show any form of desperation for gaining his business

  When I move away from the opportunity, i.e. act as if it is not that important - he moves towards me and wants the service. His ego doesn't allow him to let go – particularly if he thinks you are not interested in him. (This is a skill I have developed over years, and it takes huge confidence and bravado to pull it off – not recommended for a new starter to telephone selling unless you are great with psychology – and you can afford to turn away business)

• No sale - chosen another supplier

- When told no sale – which is not often – I am surprised - as I am not often in a competitive situation – it is more often a change in circumstances.

- Sometimes there is no sale because I qualify myself out of the opportunity because neither I, nor my services, match the decision criteria set

- Prospects more often become elusive rather than tell me no (I probably terrify most of them). But I chase him because it is important to know why - may be a little annoyed because of the time spent on the sales activity - but these are just 'thoughts in my head' - it's my own fault for not qualifying better - of course I can 'talk myself out of my annoyance'. So, I am still positive enough to accept he always has a choice, and has a right to exercise it

- I ask why he chose another company and about the differences in the services in relation to the training objectives set – my questioning may help him influence himself that perhaps his decision isn't so bright after all – I never, make any comment about the competitor's offering – he must contrast for himself and make his choice

- He may tell me its price - I never focus on the money - I never discount (I have already told him this but of course he doesn't choose to believe it)

- If he should mention a negotiation - I always tell "I am happy to increase the fees if he doesn't think he's paying enough" - he usually laughs in disbelief - I explain that I do not understand the concept that one customer pays more or less than another for the same quality service - he can just buy more or less of the service to meet his budget criteria – or I will ask him to find more money if he truly values my training

- If prospect happy with his decision - I wish him well - keep in touch for other opportunities

- If I 'know' he really and absolutely means 'no' - I cannot persuade him around - make him laugh - I close the call - keep the company on a list for a future and/or may find another contact in the organization

**Calls to
existing
customers**

A call to an existing customer is easier

Those customers who are long term, almost friends - will be sociable - chat about their children any interest or hobby – only if they have the time - if not, and with all other customers:

- I get straight to the point - discuss current needs - close on opportunities found

- Cross selling – I seldom check for opportunities to cross sell – they are in virtually every conversation if I listen actively – and when you have a great relationship with customers - these are more likely offered or directly requested - I will fulfill those I can, if not - give them another contact name and number

  - If offered a new contact in same company

  - I ask to be transferred

  - Always use existing contact as the referral point – i.e. this becomes the reason for the call, better still if I am transferred my contact explains who I am and how I can help this new contact

  - For the rest of the call I would use exactly the same process as previously described

The Art Of Telephone Selling *Spiced With The Magic Of Neuro-Linguistic Programming*

Cancellation of services

I have never had contracts with any of my customers they are free to use/not use my services as they see fit, so in this sense there is no cancellation of the service.

There are terms by which they have to give notice to cancel or transfer a committed programme but no other formal written contract.

- I have very long standing relationships with some customers, we are loyal and committed to each other – I have a great contribution to make to their staff's personal development – also improving their productivity and profit – they make a contribution to my personal development and financial well being – my profits – win/win

- When customers move away from using my services it is often because I have encouraged them to do so…if I think they are in need of fresh ideas and approaches

- This not being the case, should any of them not wish to work with me anymore this is fine, I go out and find new ones - it is not personal - it doesn't affect me emotionally - I move on - this is freedom – my highest value in life – I love variety and something new

- I have also been known to 'fire' a few of my customers too - those who continuously make late payments - particularly those I find who pay 'lip service' to training their staff

- Cold calling and selling process starts over - I love the hunt

Beliefs and values

What do I believe about myself when I am telephone selling and what is important to me and why?

- I believe I excel at influencing, be that on the telephone or face to face

- A much stronger belief - that I am an excellent trainer, and passionate about it - this is what my prospects/customers buy, and this belief and passion has a greater influence on the outcomes and my success than my actual selling skills – which are great but not phenomenal

- I am absolutely convinced I can deliver changes in behaviour when people choose to change, and prospects/customer hear this in my responses when I am selling to them

Even stronger beliefs:

- That people only buy from people they like i.e. people who are like them (not everyone likes me or my training style and this is ok – its about choice and rapport)

- There is enough work in the world for everyone, I only need enough work sufficient to fulfil my needs and desires and for those I love and support – I believe in abundance

- Co-operation and sharing is the key to freedom, peace of mind and happiness in business and life

- Money is only a by-product of doing something well...using your gifts/talents for the benefit of others

- What is important to me is that the prospects and customers 'believe' training is important for the mental well being of their staff - that I can make a valuable contribution in respect of this - that they as the employer will value both when the programme is complete

- Why is this important – freedom above all else in every context of my life and my life's work – freedom to be who I am - freedom to work with all types of people– freedom to travel where I like – freedom from emotional stresses of being told what to do - to help and support other people achieve their freedom, enjoy a quality life and have peace!

The Art Of Telephone Selling Spiced With The Magic Of Neuro-Linguistic Programming

Identity

Who am I when
telephone selling

- Free spirit
- Intuitive
- Highly self motivated
- Happy and positive
- A hunter
- Extremely assertive bordering on aggressive
- Sometimes hard (hot) headed and very single minded
- Very shrewd
- Focused business minded thinking
- Determined
- Excellent time keeper
- Disciplined
- Tenacious
- Highly organized

When making calls – is connected with the prospect in the conversation 'only my mind' immersed in the call.

For the purpose of interest in respect of 'adding the spice of NLP' my internal representations (IRs) are auditory tonal – sounds, and lots of self-talk – sometimes temperature plays a part. These particular preferences work for me, and over the years I have no doubt unconsciously tested, refined and aligned them to my understanding and use of the telesales call structure.

In a telesales context I exhibit the following traits:

Motivation traits:

- Proactive
- Towards with a little away from
- Highly internal
- Options with some procedure
- Difference

Her convincers about her prospects are:

- Hear - Do - Read

Working traits

- General only uses specific when is matching training solution to need

Her decision factors for closing on her prospects

- Automatic – when an existing customer, and real need and opportunity presents itself

- Period of time – used only as dictated by the prospects buying process

Part six

Focus
On
Success

Perfecting The Art Of Telesales *Spiced With The Magic Of Neuro- Linguistic Programming*

Focus on success

It is said that the only time 'success comes before work' is in the dictionary

I have also learned in my life that being successful is about choice. Every moment, you make a choice – i.e. you and I are where are because of the choices we have made in the past. The choice you make today will determine your future. With each choice you make, ask yourself, "Where will this choice lead? How will it affect my life tomorrow, next week, next month, 5 years from now?"

Successful people aren't any luckier, nor are they any more intelligent, or more skilled than the average person. Successful people are distinguished by the fact that they have chosen to do the things that will make them successful. Not just in the big decisions, but also the every day, moment-by-moment decisions that make up the bulk of living.

This section covers:

1. Self-preparation

2. Understanding the keys to success

The last section provides:

3. Forms and checklists to assist with your organization

4. Self-appraisal checklist to monitor your learning and development

5. Book List

There are no right or wrong ways to do telephone selling.

Some of my methods may work for you some may not; some will be more effective than others.

The efficiency of your calls will make for future success.

This guidebook is about the best practices that I found worked for me.

Refine them to work for you.

Keep what does work, and improve on it.

Change what does not.

Compare and contrast all the time.

I trust this information will help you with your continued self-awareness and learning.

Once you are aware and pay attention to what you are doing, you will become more conscious of what works and what does not.

The Art Of Telephone Selling *Spiced With The Magic Of Neuro-Linguistic Programming*

Be a bright and shining star

Success in life is self–determined.   Success in telephone selling is too.

Telephone selling skills are learned; what is required is high degree of self-motivation, determination, self-belief, tenacity, perseverance and a 'can do' mentality.

As with all professions, it requires from time to time that you assess yourself and decide what you need to improve.

If you are new to telephone selling, then you are a **new star** (low skill/low motivation), so building skill, confidence and motivation are going to be the keys to opening the door to your telephone selling success and moving towards… becoming a rising star.

If you are already a **rising star** (low skill/high motivation), meaning you have been in telephone selling a while, are successful, and want to do better, then you can improve your techniques and learn other strategies that will assist you in achieving even greater success…thus moving you towards becoming the bright star that you really are.

As a **bright star** (high skill/high motivation) you want to continue to be so, you already observe what techniques and strategies work well for you, and you keep repeating those patterns. However, in the areas that need improvement, you are motivated to learn new techniques for improving and maintaining your stardom and to move away from becoming a …fallen star and in a dilemma.

If you are a **fallen star** and in a dilemma (high skill/low motivation), this may mean you have been in telephone selling as a profession for a long time and you are feeling jaded, unsuccessful and you have lost direction. You can set about using new tools, techniques and strategies to re-focus your attention on how you used to be – a bright star.   All you need is renewed belief in yourself, and the motivation to change.
So, review the strategies you used to employ, your values, beliefs, attitudes - and most of all, what it is you really want.

The Art Of Telephone Selling *Spiced With The Magic Of Neuro-Linguistic Programming*

Skill and motivation grid

BRIGHT STAR	HIGH MOTIVATION	RISING STAR
Strategy: - Highly developed teleselling skills - Determined and highly self- motivated - Strong values and self - belief **Tactics:** - High frequency of relevant and worthwhile activity - Has harnessed talents - Uses techniques that work		**Strategy:** - Developing teleselling skills - Self-motivated - Developing self-belief and confidence **Tactics:** - Learns to improve skills - Pushes hard for results - Sets meaningful targets for self - Varies the telesales styles, is flexible and is prepared to change tactics when they are not working
HIGH SKILL ←		→ **LOW SKILL**
FALLEN STAR		**A STAR IS BORN**
Strategy: - Re-focus **Tactics:** - Faces issues which are creating de-motivation - Decides new ways to behave - Sets new strategies - Reviews and changes values, beliefs and attitudes to the job - Takes responsibility for change - Takes action	**LOW MOTIVATION**	**Strategy:** - Building teleselling skills **Tactics:** - Has a detailed and structured way of working - Building skill as a way to improve, develop and maintain motivation - Needs strong standards of performance & ways to review - Initially more focused on the hygiene factors

The Art Of Telephone Selling *Spiced With The Magic Of Neuro-Linguistic Programming*

The six  to telephone selling success

1. Believe in yourself, your product/service and your prospect

2. Know your outcome – what is it that you really want?

3. Take action – appropriate, relevant and meaningful

4. Have sensory awareness - notice the results – and change what does not work – repeat what does

5. Adjust behaviour – be flexible

6. Operate from a physiology and psychology of excellence – always (the state of your body affects the state of your mind and vice versa)

The first key means:

-   Always having belief in yourself, your product/service and your prospect

-   Belief in what you can do

-   Planning your goals in life

-   Planning for success

-   Understanding you

-   Checking what you say to yourself. Is it positive or negative? Make it positive

-   Checking what you think. Do you think resourceful thoughts?

-   Developing a 'mental' thick skin – let any rejection bounce off you!

-   Mixing with positive thinking people

The second key is having a strategy for **knowing and achieving what you want** - to become a super successful telesales person and a bright, shining star.

Focusing on an outcome that you do want creates a more engaging commitment, thus creating more certainty of your success.

If you avoid making choices for yourself in any aspect of your life, not just telephone selling, then by default, someone else will make them for you.

Do have a plan for achieving what you want.

The Art Of Telephone Selling Spiced With The Magic Of Neuro-Linguistic Programming

Gaining what you want!

A planning formula for choosing, deciding and motivating yourself:

1. **What specifically do you want? What is your goal? State it in positive language:**

   a) State **what you want** rather than what you don't want

   b) Every time you focus on what you can't do or don't want you are creating a negative outcome, and reminding yourself of what you want to avoid

   For example: You know when you say to a child "Don't touch the fire!"[1] he immediately touches it. A more useful instruction is "The fire is hot, please stay away from it". This of course takes longer to say, but the language is a positive request and not a command.

2. **Be specific in describing your goal:**

   a) In what situations do you want this goal?
   b) Where, when, how and with whom do you want it?
   c) Use as many questions as you can to check how specific you are being

3. **How will you know when you have it?**

   a) What will be the evidence that you have achieved what you want?
   b) What will you see, hear, feel or sense when you have it?
   c) To enhance the energy of your outcome and make it a reality, it is useful to imagine as much sensory-based evidence as you can. This will increase your motivation too

   E.g. In telephone selling:

   - I'll see that I'll receive at least one £xxxx order every day
   - I'll hear the customer say 'yes' to me when I ask for the order
   - I'll feel confident and relaxed about approaching my calls
   - The prospect will see the value of my product/service. They will hear words of encouragement from me, and they'll feel I acknowledge and value their needs. They will know what I am saying makes sense, and buy from me today

---

[1] "Don't" This negation used in language will, for about 85% of the population be a command, because the conscious mind cannot process a negative in consciousness. Meaning, in order to make sense of what is being said, a person has to go through the process of doing what you have just said 'don't' do. So the very thing you wish someone to avoid, they focus on, and act out. "Don't look round now but..." is another example. What does the person do? Look round.

The Art Of Telephone Selling *Spiced With The Magic Of Neuro-Linguistic Programming*

4. Is this goal within your power to achieve?

a) Is this goal self-initiated and self-maintained?   Is it only for you?
b) Are the things that you need to change within your control?
c) Be aware of whether you are dependent on someone else for your success. In this context, you are your prospect

5. How does this goal fit in with other aspects of your working life?

a) Are there other people/factors to take into account?
b) When you achieve this goal how will you really feel about it?
c) What will this goal obtain for you or allow you to do?
d) Is it representative of whom and what you want to be?
e) Is it worth what it may take to get it?

6. What are the consequences of achieving your goal?

a) For what purpose do you want this?
b) What will you gain or lose if you have it?
c) What will happen if you get it?
d) What won't happen if you get it?
e) What will happen if you don't get it?
f) What won't happen if you don't get it?

7. Extra questions you will need to ask yourself:

a) What resources are needed? There are physical and emotional types You need to remember your emotional resources (confidence, motivation, determination and so on) are inside you
b) What resources do you have now?
c) Which ones do you need to get your goal?
d) Have you ever had or done this before?
e) Do you know anyone who has?

8. Act as if you have achieved it already

Well-formed goals need to be reviewed and revised regularly for ongoing achievement. An easy way for you to remember them is to also make them SMARTER, you may have seen this mnemonic before:

Specific

Measurable

Achievable

Realistic

Time-bound

Exciting

Recorded and reviewed

Complete your own well-formed goal checklist

"I am a resourceful and successful telesales person"

1. **Stated in the Positive**
   (What specifically do I want?)

2. **Be specific**
   (In what situations do I want it? where, when, how and with whom do I want it?)

3. **How will I know when I have it?**
   (What will I see, hear, feel and sense when I have it?)

4. **Is it in my power to achieve?**
   (Is if self-initiated and self-maintained? Is it only for me?)

5. **How does this goal fit in with other aspects of my working life?**
   (What will this outcome get for me or allow me to do?)

The Art Of Telephone Selling *Spiced With The Magic Of Neuro-Linguistic Programming*

6. What are the consequences of my achieving this goal?
  (For what purpose do I want this?)

  a) What will I gain or lose if I have it?

  b) What will happen if I get it?

  c) What won't happen if I get it?

  d) What will happen if I don't get it?

  e) What won't happen if I don't get it?

  f) What resources are needed?

  g) What resources do I have now?

  h) Which ones do I need to get my outcome?

  i) Have I ever had or done this before?

  j) Do I know anyone who has?

  ACT as if I have it!

The Art Of Telephone Selling *Spiced With The Magic Of Neuro-Linguistic Programming*

Six keys to success:

1   Believing in yourself

2   Knowing what you want

3   **Taking Action** - Being organised, understanding the structure of the telesales call, adding the spice and making the calls are your responsibility, if you don't do it – it won't get done. The following pages provide information to help you get organised for telephone selling. There is no requirement for you to use them to be successful; however if you write down information and follow a method, it is more likely your success will become a reality.

To be successful in telephone selling you need some methodology – make up your own system, and as ever, pay attention to what works and what does not. Keep what does, change what does not.

4   Having **sensory awareness** is noticing what does or does not work during a telephone sales call. Being sensitive to your prospects behaviour, and building rapport.

5   **Behavioural flexibility** has been explained in how people access and process information, and for you to ensure you adapt your language and behaviour accordingly to maintain rapport.

6   **Operating from a physiology and psychology of excellence** is about your emotional state ....so let us overview this...

-    How do you want to feel when telephone selling?
-    What does success mean to you?
-    How much do you want success?
-    How much do you want a win/win situation for you and your prospect?

How you look after yourself and set yourself up to succeed is entirely based upon understanding that the body and mind are part of the same system. They affect each other. They are linked via your nervous system. This means you are the sum total of all of your sensory experiences to date, which presupposes that you have many resourceful, empowering experiences that you can call on at will.

These resourceful and empowering experiences can be re-lived so that you can experience times when you have been successful, motivated, confident, happy and so on. Knowing you can, and how to, access these positive emotional states at will - will make you more successful.

The Art Of Telephone Selling *Spiced With The Magic Of Neuro-Linguistic Programming*

A State Change Technique

(State = we run an external event through our internal processing. We make an internal representation (IR) of that event. That IR combines with a physiology and creates a 'state' which refers to the internal emotional state of an individual – a happy state, motivated and so on.)

Here one is a very simple technique to give you the opportunity to change your emotional state before you make your calls:

1. Which positive emotional state would be most useful for you to be in right now? (Confident/motivated/excited/cheerful)

2. Remember a time when you were feeling that way.   Recall a picture or create one of a chosen emotional state

3. Physiology: Sit/stand upright and move as if you are in your desired state. Seeing what you saw, feeling what you felt, hearing what you heard

4. Breathing: Take a deep breath and breathe out slowly with long 'ha' sound, then breathe as if you are in your desired state

5. Expression: Put an expression of relaxed confidence or high energy on your face and/or have your facial expression as if you are in your desired state

6. Inside your head, see, feel and hear a film of what you want to happen. Step into it and experience the positive feelings, sounds and pictures

7. If your mind starts to slip back, ask yourself "What is the perfect outcome/what do I want?" See, hear and feel the film running whilst you are in that state

If it is easier for you to visualise the state, then once you have brought it to mind, put a coloured ring around it, so you can bring it back at will.

You can recapture all kinds of feelings, and relive them, right here, right now. You just need to remember a powerful positive memory of that chosen state. See what you saw, feel what you felt, hear what you heard.

If necessary, you can enhance the memory by turning up the brightness or colour, contrast of the picture or the sounds, i.e. as if you were adjusting the brightness, contrast, volume on a TV screen. If you are not fully associated to the memory then act as if you step into the memory, feel the feelings and feel great about yourself.

If it is easier for you to 'feel' the state or 'hear something positive' do this first, then once you have brought this about, you may find you have a picture. Do whatever works best for you. Anyway you generate this highly charged positive state is fine.

The Art Of Telephone Selling *Spiced With The Magic Of Neuro-Linguistic Programming*

HAVE BELIEF IN YOU

YOU ARE A BRIGHT STAR

Operating from a mind of excellence and 'I can do' mentality will take you beyond your wildest dreams.

A desire to succeed far outstrips ability, knowledge or skills. Attitude is all.

An attitude is a belief in action. Have belief in yourself.

You have to have absolute belief that you are a successful telephone sales person, and a bright shining star

I DID	Is a word of achievement
I WON'T	Is a word of retreat
I MIGHT	Is a word of disappointment
I CAN'T	Is a word of defeat
I OUGHT	Is a word of duty
I TRY	Is a word each hour
I WILL	Is a word of beauty

I CAN   ARE WORDS OF POWER

(Source: anon)

The Art Of Telephone Selling Spiced With The Magic Of Neuro-Linguistic Programming

Part seven

Forms
&
Booklist

Forms to help with self preparation:

Book list
Other guides by this author

Perfecting The Art Of Telesales Spiced With The Magic Of Neuro- Linguistic Programming

Checklist for successful telesales calls

DID I	Yes	No	Maybe	Needs improvement	Need help with
Plan my call?					
Give a good introduction and reason for the call					
Use MANDACT effectively?					
Find sufficient and relevant information?					
Qualify all the decision makers and key influencers?					
Ask sufficient, appropriate and open questions?					
Introduce questions smoothly?					

Perfecting The Art Of Telesales *Spiced With The Magic Of Neuro-Linguistic Programming*

Actively listen to the response?				
Use the information given?				
Understand the needs/wants/desires plans?				
Confirm the needs and their priority with my prospect?				
Summarise understanding, and put over sales points enthusiastically?				
Link the features of my product/service with relevant benefits?				

Build a staircase to agreement?			
Let the prospect talk more than 50% of the time?			
Use testimonials to best effect?			
Talk in terms of you and your?			
Overcome objections successfully?			
Quote the price without fear and gave relevant benefits?			
Picked up on buying signals?			
Obtained a decision in my favour?			

Check seriousness of decision? (Remember if you have to call back get a commitment of some kind – set an expectation of his participation – this will be the reason for the follow-up call)			
Asked for the order?			
Get the business			
Not get the business – ask why?			
Leave door open for future opportunities and call backs?			

What do I need to organise/do before the next calling day?

Other comments

Call Sheet When Telephone Selling

Date:

Company Name	Contact Name	Comments	Sales today £	Not available	Send details	No Interest	Call back date

Perfecting The Art Of Telesales Spiced With The Magic Of Neuro-Linguistic Programming

Call contact Record

Date

Company Name		
Spoke to		
Job Title		
Call objective		
Questions to ask		
Outcome of call Action on prospect Action on you		
Information sent:		
Comments		
Next actions By When:		Call back date Time

Perfecting The Art Of Telesales *Spiced With The Magic Of Neuro-Linguistic Programming*

Prospecting results record

Date: Start Time: Finish Time: Total time:

Number of companies contacted	
Number of diallings	
Number of presentations	
Information to send and call back	
No needs at present and call back	
Not available	
Not interested. Why?	
Specials	
Next calling date is	Remember to diarise call backs

Sales made today:

Customer name:	Product/service bought:	£
Total sales		£

Monthly Pipeline Activity & Forecast

Date:

Company name	Contact Name	Job Title	*D M Or I	Needs/ Wants	Benefits Required	Suggested product or service	Budget Allocated	Competition or Opposition	Value to me	Comments / Decisions	Next Action dates	% S1=100 S2=70 S3=50

* Decision maker or influencers

This month Total:

S1 - 100% Committed order on the way

S2 - 70% Order likely in next month

S3 - 50% Decision not made

Perfecting The Art Of Telesales Spiced With The Magic Of Neuro-Linguistic Programming

Books I recommend you read, and some I make reference to in this guidebook

Title	Author/s
Alpha Leadership	Robert B. Dilts, Ann Deering & Julian Russell
Sleight of Mouth	Rober Dilts
Coach to Awakener	Robert B. Dilts
Dynamic Learning	Robert B. Dilts and Todd Epstein
Frogs into Princes	Richard Bandler and John Grinder
Influencing with Integrity	Gene Laborde
Instant Rapport	Michael Brooks
Magic of NLP Demystified	Byron A. Lewis & Frank Pucelik
NLP in 21 Days	Harry Alder and Beryl Heather
NLP The Technology of Achievement	Steve Andreas and Charles Faulkner
Presenting Magically	Tad James & David Shepherd
7 Habits of Highly Effective People	Stephen Covey
The Structure of Magic I & II	John Grinder and Richard Bandler
Using Your Brain For A Change	Richard Bandler
Whispering In The Wind	John Grinder & Carmen Bostic St. Clair
Words That Change Minds Mastering the Language Of Influence	Shelle Rose Charvet

OTHER GUIDE BOOKS PUBLISHED BY THIS AUTHOR

"A Practical Guide To The Art of Objection Handling"" ISBN 0 9519019 6 6
(revised and enlarged edition) © Brenda Spiller 2003

Visit the Charles Books website at: www.charlesbooksco.co.uk

Perfecting The Art Of Telesales *Spiced With The Magic Of Neuro-Linguistic Programming*